The Quiet Shift

Navigating Through the Emotional and Economic Impact of Aging Parents in the Family

Dr. Nicole B. Simpson, CFP®

Sharon Stanford

SPECIAL NOTE: To all corporations, universities, colleges, higher learning, religious and professional organizations: Quantity discounts are available on bulk purchases of this book for educational, gift purposes or as premiums for increasing magazine subscriptions or renewals. For additional information please contact **www.nicolebsimpson.com**

Simpson & Stanford

THIS IS A WRITTEN WORK BY
NICOLE B. SIMPSON & SHARON STANFORD
PUBLISHED BY HARVEST WEALTH PUBLISHING LLC

This is a book based on the divinely inspired thoughts of Nicole B. Simpson & Sharon Stanford. All content therein written as recalled and recounted by her. All identities are used by permission or purposely omitted to protect the privacy of those living or dead.

The Quiet Shift

Copyright© November 2022
By Nicole B. Simpson & Sharon Stanford

Published in the United States of America by
Harvest Wealth Publishing LLC 2022
An imprint of Harvest Wealth Publishing LLC

All rights reserved under International Copyright Law. Contents and cover may not be reproduced in whole or in part in any form without the author or publisher's written consent.

Unless otherwise indicated, all scripture quotations are taken from the King James Version of the Bible. The author has emphasized some words within the scripture quotations. These words are not emphasized in the original text.

www.NicoleBSimpson.com

Library of Congress Cataloguing-In-Publication Number
PENDING

ISBN 978-8-9871782-0-1

First Edition Printing
Printed in the United States of America
January 2023

Harvest Wealth Publishing LLC
371 Hoes Lane Suite 200
Piscataway, NJ 08854

Dedication

This book is dedicated to every family committed to leaving a legacy of love, commitment, and resources to the next generation and to my family who maintains unwavering support for every God entrusted assignment I pursue to honor.
Dr. Nicole B. Simpson, CFP®

This book is dedicated to my mom and dad, Leonard and Sylvena Stanford. I also want to include my clients and their families who trusted Stanford Angels LLC. Our Angels were allowed to come into their homes to show compassion to their loved ones.
Ms. Sharon Stanford

Dr. Simpson's Acknowledgements

This book would not exist if I never met Ann or Susan. Thank you for trusting me with your parents over two decades ago. You still trust me today and I am humbled. I want to thank my children Jesse IV and Emani who would pause their lives to care for me if needed. I have the most amazing spiritual parents, Overseer George M. Jones, and Evangelist Beverly Allen. They advise, pray, and support me with every endeavor. Reverend DeForest Soaries, Jr., I am eternally grateful for your words of encouragement and for setting me straight about how I show up in the world. Thank you, Anika J. Applewhite, for telling my story.

To my sister Sonji K. Grandy, I love you to life and my riders Fern Hazelwood and Trena Hill. To Optimism, aging looks brighter because of you. Thank you for the joy you have brought to my life.

I could not accomplish this task without Rev. Dr. Angel 'OJ' Thompson, CEO of The LEGNA Agency LLC., who makes certain that everything about me is presented well. I am appreciative to every individual who served as my focus group, answering my many questions about their family dynamics. I am grateful for your critical feedback.

Finally, a very special thank you to my contributing author Sharon Stanford. You have lit a fire when the embers of purpose were fading fast. After twenty years of desiring to address legacy planning, I met you and we were able to create magic together. Thank you for sharing this vision. I will forever appreciate your yes.

Dr. Nicole B. Simpson, CFP®

Ms. Stanford's Acknowledgements

Thank you to my three wonderful children, Amanda Budhram, Monicka Budhram, and Annasia Stanford. A special thank you to my brother Ray Stanford who has supported me through all the good and bad times in my life and encouraged me to write and complete this book. I love and appreciate every one of you.

Finally, I am sending a special thank you to Dr. Nicole B. Simpson, for allowing me to collaborate with you on this amazing and life-changing project. I am humbled and honored to be included in this part of your journey to free and empower people.

Ms. Sharon Stanford

Table of Contents

Foreword	9
Introduction	17
Caregivers' Lives Matter	29
When Life Ain't Fair	55
Dear Daddy, It's Me Jessica	81
Role Reversals	95
To Thine Own Self Be Kind	119
My Children Are My Retirement Plan	131
Doing Everything Right	153
Falling Short	163
A Final Act of Love	175
About the Authors	180

Foreword

This past week I have had a few experiences that have punctuated the value of Dr. Nicole Simpson's work and the importance of this book. The first one was a car accident. I stopped at a shopping mall to eat lunch and had a car accident that ruined the tires and rims on the right side of my car. The inconvenience was significant, and the damage was costly. Fortunately, I did not incur or cause any physical injury. And fortunately, I was prepared for the eventuality of something like this happening.

First, I have ample car insurance to assist in paying for the repairs to the car should I choose to file a claim. And I will decide whether I will file a claim rather than pay for the repairs because this car is owned by one of my businesses. It may be more beneficial financially for the business to pay the repair expense rather than having the insurance company cover the cost. But having these options results from having made many mistakes in my early years and getting good advice that I implemented in my later years. The advice I received came from professionals who in many instances, never knew me or never knew they were advising me. And many of those advisors were financial professionals like Dr. Nicole Simpson.

After having the car accident, I was able to have a tow truck take the car and me to a repair facility to assess the damage and hopefully do the repairs. My AAA membership was paid in full. That membership is paid in advance because I never want to have a problem and discover that my membership has lapsed. Given the amount of car accidents, potholes, and possible mechanical challenges I assume that a need for AAA is not a luxury but rather a necessity. That perspective causes me to include the cost of AAA membership in my budget. But the very idea of having a budget and that the likelihood of achieving wealth is enhanced by living with a budget is a lesson I learned from people like Dr. Nicole Simpson.

When I decided where to have the tow truck take my car, I identified a nearby business that quickly became the location of choice. The key to making that decision was that this business was authorized to represent the companies that make the items I would need to complete the repairs on my car. The word authorized meant that the business was qualified to handle my situation and had been approved by people that understand the nature of needs like mine. This is really the main point that relates to Dr. Simpson and her work. I have learned that we need to get instruction and advice concerning our finances from people as "authorized" or qualified as the people that we trust in other areas of our lives.

We have expectations and standards for almost every area of our lives. Our barbers and beauticians are licensed to take care of our beauty needs. Our physicians are licensed to address our healthcare needs. Pilots that fly us to our destinations are not just people that like to fly but they are trained and licensed to fly an aircraft. Training and credentials are everyday prerequisites and assumptions in our everyday lives. We should have the same standards and expectations with our personal finances. That idea is why Dr. Nicole Simpson and Sharon Stanford are such important resources to our community. They are particularly important resources as we consider the specific matter of handling the needs of aging family members. Our considerations require instructions from

The Quiet Shift

experts, who are qualified and credentialed professionals.

And that leads me to the other experience that I have had this week. My siblings and I were on a conference call concerning the care of my 91-year-old mother. My brother, sister and I have ten earned degrees between us from institutions of higher learning. My younger brother is a college professor with a doctoral degree and two master's degrees; my younger sister is a corporate attorney with a law degree and a Master of Business degree; and I am a retired pastor, corporate director, and former Secretary of State of New Jersey. Yet with all our experience and education, we have been like preschool students as it has related to managing the issues and information that our mother is facing as she is no longer physically capable of functioning independently.

Her physical health including the myriad of prescription drugs, her financial needs, her emotional well-being, and her interaction with government agencies are all so intense that we could use full-time personnel just to coordinate everything for her. It is shameful how difficult it is to age with grace and dignity in America. It is almost as if the blessing of aging is accompanied by the curses of chaos, confusion, and mean-spirited, arrogant bureaucrats who never intend to get old themselves. We needed a person with the training and expertise of Sharon Stanford who has answers for questions that we didn't even know existed.

The only part of this ordeal is that as Christians and clergy, we are prepared for end-of-life issues and are not intimidated by the reality that mom's time with us is limited. I cannot imagine having to keep our mother hopeful and emotionally healthy while also having difficult conversations about the end of life and final arrangements at the same time. Thank God the challenging aspects of those matters are well understood.

What becomes extremely challenging at moments like these is planning for the ultimate while managing the immediate.

This book is a manual that can guide individuals and families through this maze of complexity and cloud of uncertainty about inevitable life issues. There is no question that we will all have to adjust in life. The only question is whether we have prepared properly for life's swift transitions. Having a resource like this book positions us to make the needed preparations.
It is prudent and advisable to be guided through these discussions by experts who are qualified and experienced. We have the good fortune of having such individuals in these gifted authors

whose shared wisdom can be life-changing. Thank God for Dr. Nicole B. Simpson and Sharon Stanford for their foresight and willingness to empower us with their knowledge.

Reverend DeForest B. Soaries, Jr.
Pastor Emeritus of First Baptist Church of Lincoln Gardens
Central Jersey Community Development Corporation
Harvest of Hope Family Services Network, Inc.

Introduction

Meet Nicole

The moment I became a Certified Financial Planner over twenty years ago, the first area of concern that I wanted to specifically address was long-term care. I didn't realize the impact of caring for an aging parent would have such a detrimental impact on the entire family until I broadened my business focus beyond stocks and bonds. Wet behind the ears, I was still a novice. Although I was educated in the arenas of investments and comprehensive planning, I realized immediately that the dynamics of wealth accumulation shifted drastically in the minority communities as the senior citizens I admired economically began to transition. The thread was a common one. They would maintain a decent lifestyle by buying a house, driving a nice car, going on vacations, and dressing well. The surface, visible definition of being financially secure. As they grew older, they would get sick and die broke. You would see the deterioration of the home structure and in the 21st century, the era of social media, a Go Fund Me account would be established to beg for the money to handle the final expenses. The aftermath was even more brutal. Personal property and tangible assets were divided or retrieved from the home, yet very few people had taken the time to establish wills. The bills could not be maintained and in a short period of time, the most valuable financial and sentimental asset in the family- the primary residence- would be lost. I would despairingly witness generational wealth elude the families time and time again. I was compelled to break that cycle. So, I began to write.

I was thirty years old, working at 2 World Trade Center, looking to make an economic mark in the African American community. I was young, eager, and ready. I had impressive credentials and a ten-year track record, which yielded me a reputation as one who worked hard in the securities industry. I began my career working in operations as a new accounts clerk and a backup wire operator, meaning I opened brokerage accounts and entered trade orders for financial advisors. Once I got my foot in the door, I began to study for my Series 7 license. I didn't understand the significance at that time, but I had an amazing mentor whom I trusted immensely. He guided me through the first leg of my career. At the tender age of twenty-one, I passed the exam on my first attempt. Now that I was registered, I petitioned for the opportunity to move from what was called the back office, to be on the floor. I secured a position as a registered sales assistant. I went on to acquire my Series 63, Series 65, and Series 3 (which I allowed to lapse when I decided to pursue financial planning) and ultimately my life and health insurance license before I obtained the coveted CFP® credentials. Within that first ten-year window, I gleaned from multiple financial advisors who were successfully focusing on different areas of wealth accumulation. It was after the birth of my second child, that I began to focus on building my client base in an industry that I had grown to love and was flourishing in. Working with families that I met allowed me to see beyond building a financial plan for abstract client number 142. I became a trusted advisor to everyone who gave me a chance to help them build a strategic plan to improve their economic quality of life.

The reason why I wanted to write a book was simple. The purpose was to educate families about the impact caring for an aging family takes on the entire family over time. Then 9/11/01 happened and I lost everything, including my working manuscript. I was literally

The Quiet Shift

on the 73rd floor of 2 World Trade Center working in my office when Tower 1 was struck. I made it to the 44th floor when Tower 2 was attacked. Fortunately, I survived the ordeal, but my mission had changed. I could not afford to stay the course and write about what I originally intended. The objective was delayed, but never abandoned. It stayed with me, and over the course of the twenty years since September 11th, 2001, I recognized that writing about the challenges families endured while caring for an aging parent at that time would have been premature. I didn't know, what I didn't know at the tender age of thirty. Today, I am equipped with personal knowledge, sweat equity, and the expertise to validate my perspective. Additionally, I am not taking this all-important journey to educate and empower all families alone. I have enlisted the support and expertise of Sharon Stanford.

In our families, we represent the first generation of wealth accumulators and incidentally, we are both identified as Generation X. When I met her and she shared her vocation with me, I immediately said, "*Oh my goodness, you have to write this book with me.*" I knew there was a connection between the emotional toil that was being heavily leveraged on our age demographics and the lack of wealth that was not being transferred from one generation to the next. What exactly was I missing? How can I break the cycle and what could I possibly say that would reverberate throughout multiple generations? Sharon saw a need and decided to establish a home health care agency recognizing families who needed support when caring for aging parents. She understood it went beyond critical care. In the capacity of her vocation, she saw firsthand the response from all parties involved. That is what was missing. The truth about how families engage with each other when a family member gets older becomes chronically ill or suffers a devastating injury. The impact is felt by everyone involved. One additional consideration, I have studied our emotional connections to money, the attitude of people, their thought processes concerning money, and the decisions they make. It is something I felt was critical in engaging with our community and it has fared well over the years. I bring that perspective to the table as well.

Meet Sharon

As the saying goes, "If you love what you do, you will never work a day in your life." I wholeheartedly believe that to be true. During my childhood I watched my mother take pride in helping and caring for others as a nurse. Although I admired my mother and her work ethic, I never intended on following in her footsteps. Like most teenagers after graduating,

I had no idea what I wanted to do with my life. Just winging it was not an option especially coming from a strict Caribbean background as I did. You had to do something, have a clear direction you wanted to go in life, set a goal, and begin to pursue it. Wandering around aimlessly without a plan simply did not work. When I didn't land anywhere after a set period, my mother strongly encouraged me to take a healthcare class just to see if I would like it. I did, but I was still somewhat hesitant. It was upon completing that class and landing my first "real job" taking care of an elderly man that I realized not only did I love taking care of people, but I was also really good at it. I had found my landing pad. It wasn't nursing, but it was my way to serve.

I didn't just stop there, after realizing my passion I decided that I wanted to further my education in the medical field. Life has a way of

The Quiet Shift

taking turns we never anticipate. I made the commitment to pursue my certifications in the medical field and then I turned around and switched industries. I know, it would have been logical to jump right into the medical field and continue pursuing my passion- but not Sharon. At the approximate age of twenty-two, I changed my mind and began a career in the automotive industry, honing and cultivating customer service skills that I would eventually need in my life. While it appeared to be starkly different, I needed that deviation in my life at that season.

I had children to raise and that required money. At that time the automotive industry offered better wages than the healthcare industry, so I decided to pursue it. Fortunately, children grow up and eventually branch off on their own. When my children finally left, I had time on my hands. My priorities shifted and I began to realize my passion and desire to help others never waned.

What made me leave the healthcare industry initially is what drew me back with a different objective. I dared to believe I could make a difference. Many healthcare employees are underpaid and overworked dealing with vulnerable populations, senior citizens, and the chronically ill. I decided to return to my first passion and opened my healthcare agency.

With great customer service skills, a medical background, and educational credentials, I had a vision for what quality care looked like and I set out to make it a reality. Everyone hears about the mishaps and mistreatment that occur with the elderly in healthcare facilities, and I was determined to change that. It is devastating and the pressure and responsibility associated with compassionate care are already taxing on families. When you add the economic impact into the mix, it can be a recipe for disaster. I knew I couldn't manage family dynamics, but I could create a business where healthcare employees who love what they do as my mother did could provide excellent care to our elderly clients. That was my commitment. That is the reason why Sandford Angels, LLC. was established.

When Dr. Nicole expressed her desire for us to write a book together, I was excited about the possibility. My goal is to shed light on what compassionate care entails. I want people to understand the economic impact it can have on a family and we both want to ensure that readers know that we must begin to have critical conversations much sooner than later. Part of loving your family requires you to begin to address the way you desire to live in your senior years. This conversation must touch on the financial impact your care will require. Not having a plan is devastating all around and will cause families to be torn apart long after you have departed this earth.

The Intersection

Sharon and I share a common agenda, so we decided to collaborate and bring to life what we have experienced over the years. This literary journey consists of real-life experiences we both encountered over the years. The case studies we identified should resonate with you and your family dynamics. Sharon is sharing the impact that care will have under the stated conditions, and I provide the potential financial considerations and consequences with or without a strategic plan. Together we anticipate it will spark dialogue amongst beloved family members so that everyone has the economic ability to accumulate, preserve and ultimately transfer wealth. The most egregious mistake

The Quiet Shift

families commonly make is planning for the eventual transition of life. The truth is that all humans born into this world will eventually die. When that happens, what is your plan?

Caregivers Lives Matter

I recall getting a phone call asking for my assistance. The family led with the news that would capture the attention of any investment advisor. The woman on the phone said, "My son Tyson is the recipient of a lawsuit and I need help." Almost immediately, I made the decision not to ask the question that most people in my position want to hear to determine how much time to commit to the cause. Truth is that there was something in the woman's voice, a tremble and I could hear the sense of desperation seeping out with each word. Turns out, an egregious medical error caused a young man to become permanently paralyzed just as he entered his young adult years. In addition to being incapable of walking, his mental capacity was deeply affected resulting from being administered too much anesthesia. The lack of oxygen caused brain damage and just like that, the young, strapping male who had a bright future was now confined to a wheelchair and incapable of caring for himself.

Shocked, the family didn't know what to do. It took them years to fight the hospital for a settlement and the design of the settlement payout further compounded the economic damage levied upon the family. Let me explain. It took almost 5 years of going back and forth in the court system to determine what would be fair or just compensatory damages. After five years of going back and forth to the doctors, all family members were impacted economically. The mother, who was the original primary caregiver was advanced in age and needed her medical support and daily assistance from the children before this turn of events. Five years of fighting with attorneys trying to get the most appropriate advocate who would see the young man as someone who had his entire future snatched away. The family had no direction regarding the hidden costs to become full-time caregivers to a paralyzed man. In addition, they had no concept of how their lives, their time would no longer be their own. Everyone was impacted economically.

The family heard me speak on the lecture circuit. My topic was titled 'The Ultimate Plan'. I was traveling the country sharing about the importance of planning for life's unexpected events and how one must consider the economic impact a catastrophe could have on a family. My trauma story resonated so much that immediately following the lecture, a sibling approached me to see if I would meet everyone in the family. We exchanged sweet pleasantries and went our separate ways. When they contacted me, they brought to my recollection where we met and who they were. I agreed to visit the family. Immediately upon my arrival, I observed there were the mother and sister, whom I had previously met. A second sister was present and there were two young ladies in the room as well. One was preparing to graduate college and the second was a junior in high school.

As the evening unfolded, what became clear is that the family never received financial advice or appropriate guidance when making executive decisions on behalf of Tyson. By the time we met, three generations of the family were in financial ruin. The structure of the settlement did not take into consideration medical needs of Tyson, so the family was left trying to manage his life and theirs. The lawsuit had given them an increasing lump sum every five years and a monthly annuity that increased annually as well. The settlement was guaranteed for 30 years of Tyson's life period certain. That means that if he were to die before the end of the 30 years, the beneficiaries would receive the difference. If he lived beyond 30 years, payments would be rendered for the remainder of his life. On paper, the settlement appeared to be in the millions of dollars. Unfortunately, the medical actuarial costs were not appropriately calculated, or the attorney was focused on his portion of the settlement or because this was a minority family, they were simply taken advantage of. Whatever the reason, there were three generations living well beneath their ability to earn.

For many families like Tyson's this is not only emotionally but financially overwhelming. The level of care in a situation such as his can easily become very costly even with insurance. His care plan can consist of either a live-in nurse in the privacy of the patient's home or a long-term care facility that will take care of the patient's overall needs. If the family chooses to go with a live-in nurse which will include 24-hour/7 days a week care from a live-in nurse and/or CNA. The nurse would have to assist with ADLs (activities of daily living) such as feeding, bathing, dressing, grooming, helping the patient get in and out of bed, etc. The family would have to provide a room and food for the live-in nurse and/or CNA. The cost for a live-in nurse can range from ($13,500 -15,000 monthly) not including the cost of doctor's visits, therapy, transportation services, and prescriptions. If the family chooses to go with a long-term care facility, that alternative is even more expensive. The patient would have to turn over all financial rights to the facility. They will control all his expenses and assets, and provide round-the-clock care from CNA, LPN or RN, physical therapist, and speech and language therapist. The cost for this kind of care can range anywhere from ($ 10,000 - 20,000 monthly.)

The family was never given the chance to consider those costs. They didn't have the guidance or even the capacity to comprehend what direct care would entail. Add to the complication, everyone the family trusted, did not have their best interests, or needs at heart. In short, when the first lump sum payment was released, the decisions the family made immediately placed them in a handicapped position. A million dollars appears to be a significant amount of money, especially if one is given a check for the entire amount. In addition, a monthly distribution from an annuity would pay out $5,000 with an annual cost of living rider attached. Let's break that down in simple math. The five-year struggle to be primary caregivers exposed the first weakness of the family. The collective family decided that the children would not be hampered by the responsibility of taking care of their uncle. Both of Tyson's sisters had one daughter each. But

The Quiet Shift

his baby sister Tawana was married with responsibilities to her spouse Jacob. Her ability to be present was limited. The eldest sister Tanisha found herself carrying the weight of the caretaker responsibilities because Mrs. Johnson had underlying medical conditions and to be quite honest, she was too old to manage Tyson alone. Mrs. Johnson, Tanisha, and Tyson moved in together purchasing a home with the settlement money. The idea seemed logical. Get a 6-bedroom house in a beautiful neighborhood where they could live together comfortably. If they maintained a small mortgage on the house, the monthly distribution and Mrs. Johnson's social security and pension benefits should be sufficient to cover the costs.

But what about Tanisha? What became abundantly clear in the first year was that Tanisha could not keep a job and care for an aging parent and disabled sibling. Tawana couldn't provide much help from day to day-she had her own family to care for. If Tanisha isn't working, she isn't adding to her social security, she isn't saving and she isn't living her own life. She isn't even earning money to take care of her personal needs. Tanisha is doing a significant amount of work, with limited economic benefit. The settlement alone meant the family would not be eligible for any benefits that could eliminate the costs of quality care. So, the math that appeared ideal initially is now below the poverty level. If I get back to the math, the one million dollars was used to purchase a million-dollar home with a sizable down payment. That became necessary because the income to guarantee the mortgage was the monthly annuity and Mrs. Johnson's fixed income. That meant the house would be in the trust name for Tyson's benefit, something the attorneys advocated for as a protective measure for Tyson. That decision crippled the entire family because the money could only be touched for the care, welfare, and overall well-being of Tyson. Tanisha was stuck taking care of her brother and mother, incapable of working personally and relying upon the charity of the family. I don't even want to get into the emotional toll this can have on a family. It was purely out of family obligation that Tanisha remained honorable. In addition, she sacrificed her life to make certain her daughter would not get trapped in the vicious, unrelenting predicament.

Now that the million dollars had dwindled to approximately $400,000 after all the past bills were paid off that had been accumulating over the past five years, a wheelchair-accessible van now needed to be purchased as well. That was an estimated cost of $50,000. It quickly became abundantly clear that there was always a complication, a need that had to be met, and an expense that was unaccounted for. The family was forced to go to a predatory lender to exchange the anticipated five-year lump sum distribution that increased over time. They didn't go once; they were forced to solicit those services twice. It was just after the third payout; the family knew this was not sustainable any longer. They lived below poverty means for just over a decade being taken advantage of without help or sage advice that would significantly change the course of their lives for the better.

My heart broke because the family was not well served at all. Having said that, as the advisor, I had to break down several hard truths that all parties needed to hear, primarily Mrs. Johnson and Tawana. I found it personally fascinating that Mrs. Johnson harbored a level of resentment because she felt her life had been forever altered. One can understand the angst and it shows up too often in a family dynamic,

The Quiet Shift

but society doesn't give space for people to truly express how they feel when it appears that life is dealing a cruel blow. What is most unfortunate is that her frustration was oftentimes levied against the one ally, the primary caregiver who did her level best to provide for everyone-Tanisha. Tyson was Mrs. Johnson's son, not Tanisha's. Who should feel the greatest obligation to Tyson? As an observer, I thought Mrs. Johnson needed to understand the sacrifice Tanisha was making daily to offer everyone a better quality of life, to her own detriment. There is a presumption that people will always do what is best or right. But who gets to make that determination? Are other people not willing to make the sacrifice themselves? When one considers life from Tanisha's lens, it appears extremely insensitive to negate her feelings. She couldn't date. Every time a man expressed interest; Tanisha was forced to choose family over her happiness. It wasn't a straightforward decision she made. It showed up with missed dates, long spans at the hospital, difficult nights for both mom and Tyson, and trips to the doctor. An impromptu need here, and an *"I gotta go there"*. That level of responsibility weighs heavily upon any relationship. Who could blame a suitor?

The first thing I thought was important to address was the roles of each party. I wanted to get a full grasp on what the family had done for the previous decade and exactly what did they desire? They needed to hear from one another what was deemed a priority. I can recall discussing what should or needed to be done. No one mentioned what was best for Tanisha. I learned about Tyson and how he was suffering. They mentioned the pressure and stress Mrs. Johnson carried and how it was contributing to the deterioration of her health as she continued to age, and not very gracefully I might add. Even

The Quiet Shift

Tawana shared her grievances because every hospital visit or complication with mom's health yielded a phone call to keep her in the 'know'. No one even considered Tanisha. Tanisha was the one who kept all the records, made sure the doctors' appointments were kept, and took care of mom when mom didn't feel her best. Tanisha cooked, kept the house clean, did all the grocery shopping, and provided the family with the best care possible without murmuring and complaining. She had to account for the money and the fact that the family was continually in a deficit added further scrutiny about the judgment calls she was forced to make.

To further complicate the matter, the family did not consider that each doctor visit required a co-payment or a deductible that needed to be met. Tanisha was educated, she had skills that had nothing to do with primary caregiving and she always had the option of walking away. Here you had three grown adults living off an income of approximately $7200 each month. Placed in its proper perspective, one could see that the money coming into the household was much less than what was necessary to maintain the household. After assessing the situation and understanding where everyone stood emotionally, the next task was to stop the financial hemorrhaging. That road would prove to be far more complicated than anyone could have imagined. It was at that time I thought the family needed to pause. I simply asked a question to make everyone think. I wanted to know what they thought about Tanisha. I understand the question would be off-putting and perhaps place everyone on the defensive. Yet they needed to see that she was the lynchpin for any shift to happen. Fortunately, all parties involved recognized that if they didn't take drastic measures, each passing year would make them worse off than their present condition.

The decision to move out of the state to a state where the cost of living was not as high was the first step. In the state of New Jersey, property taxes alone averaged $12,000-$15,000 annually. The family moved to a state where property taxes were virtually nonexistent, and the value of the house was less expensive. After turning a profit on the original house, they rolled that profit into the new house and reduced their monthly housing costs to less than $1500. It was almost half of their monthly budget in New Jersey. The second step was to help Tanisha receive compensation for the quality of care she was providing to her mother, who had advanced in age and needed long-term care as well. After careful research, they chose a state who focused on a rising initiative where family members were being compensated for providing support services to people willing to deliver care at home for a senior or a disabled person. Mrs. Johnson fit the requirements.

It was still a struggle, but those two decisions accomplished two major objectives; they significantly reduced the financial hemorrhaging and they restored Tanisha's dignity without having to make the continued economic sacrifices that would destine her to a life of poverty during her most vulnerable years as a senior citizen. Sadly, that remained their financial condition until Mrs. Johnson died a decade after we met in 2005 and Tyson transitioned almost 4 years afterward just before the turn of the new decade. Tanisha did not bode well taking care of her family. If the truth is to be told, as someone currently in her mid-seventies, her options would have been extremely limited. However, she learned from experience that she had to do something, so we implemented a strategy from the moment she began receiving compensation for her mother's care.

Her saving grace throughout the entire ordeal has helped her tremendously. While she was employed as her mom's primary caregiver, Tanisha remained frugal in her spending and was able to accumulate a small nest egg. We set her up to contribute to her 401k which was connected to the institution that paid her to provide for her mom's long-term care and receive the company match. At the same time, she established a ROTH IRA and contributed the max amount available. She maintained that strategy for the entire nine years she was employed while her mother remained alive. While the daily responsibilities were minimized, she was back to square one. But now she could work outside of the home with menial jobs that offered flexibility. Tyler would now receive care for hours daily and that gave Tanisha something she had not benefited from for decades- freedom. The ability to get up and go, the chance to hop on a plane for a three or four-day sabbath. This was considered a blessing to her for the remaining time of Tyler's life. In his last year on earth, medical complications were common. It felt like he was rushed to the hospital weekly for one issue or another. Finally, in 2019, he took his last breath and Tanisha was free. I know it doesn't feel right to say she was free, but when you are a caregiver, you give up your life for the benefit of someone else's sake. It is not glamorous or pretty and sometimes it is a thankless responsibility.

The truth is that after caring for any individual for an extended period, one must learn to adjust. After all, the care person's life is oftentimes dictated by the medical schedule of the person in need. Alarms are usually the

The Quiet Shift

guide, the calendar of events must be worked around doctor appointments, and then suddenly, it's all over. Imagine doing that level of care for decades and then suddenly, it stops. When does it finally kick in? I remember asking Tanisha when her new reality hit her. I can recall her response vividly. She indicated that it wasn't until weeks past the funeral. Her internal clock was accustomed to giving out medication for set periods. One day, she slept so soundly and when she awoke and glanced at the clock, she immediately panicked. It was hours past medicine distribution. After she calmed down, she began to weep. She had no obligations, nothing to do for anyone except herself. She didn't have any appointments to keep. She didn't have to rush home. All the things she didn't have to do began to flood her mind and eventually, she began to self-reflect. What do I do now? That glaring question was difficult to process. Here is a woman, now looking at turning 70 years old as one looks down the barrel of a gun. She lived her life obligated to others and now the only person she was responsible for was herself? Did she even know how to treat herself?

When the dust settled, Tanisha was the primary beneficiary of the home she had cared for her brother and mom. Within a year of his transition, she sold the home and received a step up in the basis for the house which had appreciated greatly over time. The estate tax liability was limited, and she immediately purchased a property in her name paying cash for her piece of mind. The rationale was to secure a place where she could live for the remainder of her life without worrying about the cost of paying rent and the rent increasing to an unmanageable amount over time. While it would be customary for me to recommend a small mortgage, in her case, purchasing the house outright achieved several goals. It took away the financial anxiety she lived with her entire life. Because she was advanced in age, she didn't want to burden her daughter with her final affairs. She had never attained life insurance because of her inability to make payments consistently. With an outstanding mortgage, her greatest fear was burdening her daughter with a potential undue burden. After the purchase, she still had just shy of 300,000 dollars between her inheritance, retirement savings, and the ROTH IRA money. Because she was invested in the stock market and maintained a diversified portfolio, she was fortunate to accumulate some resources.

Tanisha isn't out of the woods economically. Once she was independent of all responsibilities, she wanted to continue to work for an additional 5-7 years, provided she remained healthy. Just when 2020 arrived,

Covid-19 hit the country and that intention was quickly squashed. The inability to work leaves her with great, uncovered risk. She doesn't have long-term care provisions for herself and therefore she runs the risk of living a life of poverty. Georgia is an income-cap state, meaning, to qualify for Medicaid if needed, her earnings cannot surpass a certain threshold. Because she only receives a small social security check, she meets the requirements. However, there is an additional stipulation that you can only have a certain amount of assets. Her small nest egg, that safety net, is in jeopardy.

The primary takeaway from this family scenario should be the importance of taking personal responsibility for your overall financial well-being. Doing the right thing to provide care for family members, both direct and extended, cannot come at the risk of maintaining self-sufficiency. I marvel at Tanisha's integrity and commitment to her family. I am not certain if given the same set of circumstances, how many people would choose her pathway and remain optimistic about their future. She acknowledges she has lost a lot. Truthfully speaking, as one ages, the ability to earn diminishes with each passing day. Living in poverty with minimum options can cause any individual to live with extreme discomfort. I am happy to say that when it was pointed out, the family responded to Tanisha with gratitude and appreciation. They were more sensitive to her feelings and less critical of the decisions she made on behalf of the family. At different intervals, they are the ones who made certain Tanisha was able to enjoy time away for rest and rejuvenation. It made things easier for all parties involved.

I want you to consider your family, mom, and dad, your children. Picture them from Tanisha's lens. Imagine if they did everything she did, but they lived in a state where taxes are extraordinarily high so they run the risk of losing their home of over forty years because they cannot pay the annual taxes. Imagine their frail frames and aching body. Think about the medication they need but cannot afford to purchase. Now consider where they will go. Most of us will do everything possible to prevent that from happening to our parents, especially while we are young, healthy, and strong. Here is the issue, without proper planning, you may prevent the scenario being your parents' final days, at the personal economic cost to your overall retirement savings. Unfortunately, you will realize it too little too late. Tanisha continues to live modestly. As soon as the vaccination became available, she went back to work on a part-time basis and remains optimistic that she will have sufficient resources to live out the remainder of her life in peace.

When Life Isn't Fair

Imagine this with me for a moment. I want you to picture this family's dynamic in real-time. It was one business relationship that I encountered where I wish I could have gone back to the birth of Amy Davenport to plead with her mom to do right by her baby girl. Amy was not the only child. She was, however, the only girl in a family of 9 where the father was a Southern Baptist preacher and the mom was deeply religious, yet bitter and angry. Therefore, this is written as if you are intruding on the varied conversations and experiences the Davenport family endured over time. I hope that it impacts every individual at the core of their existence so that you, yes you, understand how important it is to treat your family with love, honor, and respect and that you make provisions for your overall quality of care as you mature in age. The reality is that unless you die premature, you will get old. With aging, you may not age in the best of health. You may find that you need assistance and guidance even as you attempt to live a quality life. The emotional responses are real, organic, and expressed over a period of twenty-five years.

The phone rings and Amy hustles to answer it. She had left it in the living room as she went into the kitchen. So, by the time she got to the phone, it went silent. Missed call. It was "mom." Immediately she tensed up, attempting to brace herself knowing that she had approximately 5-10 minutes to return the call, or her phone would ring incessantly. Mom demanded that. After all, it had been several days since they last communicated, and Amy winced as she recalled the last encounter. Replaying in her head was her mother's wrath cloaked with scripture. Amy simply didn't feel like hearing that she was going to hell. But what was normal language still seared in her spirit as she tried to tolerate her mom as an adult.

Growing up in a household of six brothers and being the only girl was a tough break as Amy was the second-born child to John and Rebecca Davenport. John was a traveling preacher who grew up in the rural parts of Bowman, South Carolina. He was also married to the church, the women in the church, the liquor store near the church, and everything else not residing within the confines of his home. His charisma and ability to show compassion around those whom he engaged with within the community afforded him significant tolerance for his many transgressions over the years. The rules in the house and what he preached about across the pulpit were apparently for everyone else and not for Rev. Davenport. All Amy's life, she lived in an atmosphere where women were treated as second-class citizens. Her role was to serve her brothers, which meant she must cook, clean, and do whatever was necessary to make certain everyone else was well provided for. She was called to assist her mom at every turn and anytime she would murmur or complain, she would feel the wrath of her mother's angst. It was not until Amy became an adult, did she realize that many of the challenges she endured as a child and responsibilities were forced upon her because she was not male-gendered. That epiphany, although real, still paled in comparison to her mother's role and responsibilities as a preacher's wife.

Rebecca Davenport was an aging beauty. While it was clear that life didn't treat her kindly, a glimpse of what used to still exist. She thought she had it all. She met John during her freshman year at Oral Roberts University and it was a whirlwind romance. Married within a year and

The Quiet Shift

quickly impregnated, she never had an opportunity to complete school. First, there was Junior, then Amy. When Amy turned 2 years old, Dexter and Donald-fraternal twins came into the world. She thought the family was complete. Surely three pregnancies were enough. But any conversations about birth control fell on deaf ears anytime Rebecca mentioned it to John. In a total of ten years, she was pregnant six times with seven children to care for. Rounding out the numbers were Jake, Brandon, and Mark. They were the Davenports and very active in their local community.

The truth was that while it appeared that the family was tight-knit and loving, inside the four walls was a warzone for both Rebecca and Amy. To make matters worse, Amy was on the receiving end of all that needed to be managed in a traditional household, while being demoralized, disrespected, and not protected by anyone. It was clear that her father favored her, but he was never around. It was the teachings that caused her to grieve. She was forced to serve her brothers to prepare her for marriage, she was to be silent when the men were speaking, and she was constantly reminded that she was supposed to honor her father and mother in the Lord, for it was the right thing to do. The enforcer of the rules- Rebecca. Instead of having a loving mother working as an ally to protect her daughter, the only one truly supporting Rebecca with all household responsibilities, it was Rebecca who inflicted most of Amy's invisible scars.

The adage that says, "What goes on in this house, stays in this house" is extremely dangerous and unfortunately the mantra of many dysfunctional families. It makes matters worse when theological doctrine dictates one's actions, yet there is an unwillingness to

The Quiet Shift

appropriately interpret the doctrine or to see the flawed, unhealthy interpretation that marginalized or oppresses a class or group of people. The Bible has been used to manipulate and control women and the Davenport women experienced that manipulation in their household. That's why when given the chance to move out, Amy hightailed it out of the house and committed to never living there again. The school was acceptable, although she needed to remain in-state and had to return home with great regularity. Once she graduated, she seized the opportunity to find a job and apartment near her Alma Mater Southern Methodist College approximately 20 minutes away.

"Ring!" The phone rang. She answers it reluctantly knowing that she was getting ready to hear an exhausting tirade that included the myriad of ways she was an epic failure. To her surprise, the voice that met her hello was faint, weary, and barely audible. Amy immediately deduced that something was off. "What's wrong mom?" was Amy's response to her mom's faint cry of her name. Then she caught wind of the labored breathing and knew something was amiss. She jumped into action moving about swiftly, first to call 9-1-1 before rushing out of the door to her parents' house. She was trying to get her mom to speak, keeping her on the phone while she frantically drove making every effort to keep her mother alert and talking. At the same time, she was already badgering herself internally because she failed to return her mother's original call. "What if" scenarios continued to run through her mind as she prayed to God, "Please God, not like this. You can't let this happen. This isn't fair! Please let her be okay."

It is that moment when so many thoughts are going through one's head about the choices one makes and the consequences of those choices. In Amy's mind, everything was unfair again. She felt she would be blamed, that somehow it was her fault. She knew someone would ask what she was doing so important, that she couldn't answer her mother's call the first time. This was the stress and anxiety she was desperately trying to escape. Imagine someone blaming you for everything that goes on wrong in their life. Think about how you would feel if you were always the target of your family's wrath or the black sheep of the family or the one destined for hell because you are a heathen and a disappointment. Logically speaking, you know you moved away simply to reduce, not even eliminate, being the emergency contact or the one expected to drop everything and run. Your life was expendable, your dreams were irrelevant and if it didn't involve the church, it was not the Lord's plan for your life.

She pulls up into the driveway and dashes into the house hysterically calling out her mom's name to gauge her whereabouts. The moment she had turned on the block, she disconnected the call to contact 9-1-1 again to determine the arrival time of the ambulance. As she ran from room to room, she could hear the sirens getting louder and she ultimately found her mother sprawled across the bed, the telephone still in hand. She appeared delirious and she was breathing faintly. Incidentally, Amy noted that her brother Brandon's car was in his driveway, three houses down from their mom and dad. "Mom, are you okay, mom? Can you hear me?" The ambulance's arrival captured the attention of Brandon who came rushing into the house. The paramedics begin hooking Rebecca up to oxygen tanks, checking for vital signs, and making plans to transport her to the hospital.

The Quiet Shift

The hospital ride represented one of the longest periods for Amy as she watched her mom gasping for air and the doctors working on her ferociously. It felt like hours when in fact the hospital was a mere nine minutes from the house. When the entire ordeal was under control and the doctors had the chance to explain to the family what was happening with Rebecca, Amy was the first to truly understand that everyone's life was getting ready to drastically change; hers more than anyone else. Although Rebecca suffered from high blood pressure, a stroke? She was too "healthy" for that. But that was the diagnosis and because mom had been left alone for quite some time, the effects were great. She suffered a hemorrhagic stroke. The delayed treatment caused some brain damage and simply put; the lost time would have a lasting impact. The road to recovery would be long and mom would require significant quality care. Based on the family dynamics, it was assumed that Amy would become the primary caretaker for her mother's treatment. But no one consulted Amy. They didn't even take her life, her family dynamics, or anything into consideration.

While the Davenports had insurance, they did not have long-term care coverage. Rebecca's hospital expenses were rapidly piling up and she was eventually transferred to a skilled care facility. The entire family had inaccurately assumed she would be provided for because she had Medicare. They learned the hard way that Medicare would cover the first twenty days at 100% of the cost, but from day twenty-one until day one hundred, the coverage would be only 80% and they were responsible for the coinsurance. After spending 4 ½ months in the facility, Rebecca still needed major attention, but the decision was made that she needed to receive those services at home. The 100-day window for Medicare coverage had passed and the financial burden increased significantly. It was quickly realized that based on finances alone, Rebecca had to receive services from home. The challenge was that the needs were great, but the resources were not. This is a problem families face when it's too late to explore all viable options that would make any individual suffering from a physical ailment choose the best care plan available. The decision is oftentimes dictated by the funds available or lack thereof.

For starters, the Davenports weren't wealthy, but they were certainly comfortable financially. John earned a decent income provided he was able "serve the church". Being in ministry afforded them luxuries many families cannot fathom; from favorable tax breaks as clergy to tax-free financial benefits that a congregation can provide for their pastors and leaders in ministry. Oftentimes, the church is willing to help maintain a comfortable standard of living, but the benefits are often subpar. If a minister neglects to develop a financial plan or strategy for the family, they often fall miserably short when looking to accumulate and manage wealth. The impact is even greater if protection of income or earnings was never considered. The family "lived in the now" and was not appropriately prepared for an economic tsunami. There were medical bills, copayments each time a doctor needed to be contacted, prescriptions to be filled, etc., etc. Those were actual costs. Someone needed to check on Rebecca, be available for Rebecca, and meet her needs. Surely the men and Rev. John would take on some of those burdens. After all, Amy isn't a child living at home any longer and he is the one who signed up for better or worse-right? Wrong.

The Quiet Shift

It didn't even cross John's mind that the primary responsibility was his to undertake. The children were grown, and everyone led separate lives. To even place such a demand on a child is outright selfish and insensitive. Why am I saying this? Oftentimes parents assume their children "owe" them. At what point is the debt paid? It wasn't as if Amy was treated fairly or even equal to her brothers. Did she ask to be born? Did she have anything to do with the making of her gender? How long does one honor their parents when respect isn't reciprocated? Difficult questions to answer indeed, but many parents inaccurately assume their children are their long-term care plan and that is both unfortunate and the best way to leave a legacy of poverty.

When the family came to grips with their new reality that mom was incapable of taking care of herself, when they fully understood she needed long-term care and someone had to be always present, the Davenports came together to determine what could be done. It was all the men versus Amy. All the men had multiple excuses as to why they could not even be considered in the care plan. None offered the support of their spouses either. They all bullied Amy into submission. It was settled. "Amy, this is your reasonable service, and you must honor your mother for this is right in the eyes of the Lord." She never had a chance to fight for her freedom. She couldn't get the men to understand her life had meaning and that while she was willing to help, she had responsibilities as well. She had no desire to return home, put a halt on her career, or even become the primary caregiver. Never mind the fact she wanted to love and be loved, something she longed for because she felt she was lacking in that area.

Amy could have said no. She could have moved to another state. Many difficult choices were available to Amy. From a cultural and spiritual lens, effective ministry counseling was not beneficial to her because of the Davenports' positioning in the community and the mindset of their specific church theology that women were inherently inferior or tasked with typical gender roles. However, if she could have moved past the barriers set up by religious ideology, Amy could have charted a different course. Emotional abuse and manipulation over the years left Amy weak and vulnerable, incapable of finding enough internal strength to defend herself. Her feeble attempts to offer viable solutions that included shared responsibilities fell on deaf ears. She was not being heard. In my defense, I must clearly articulate that while this was a business relationship, the Davenports were not my clients, although they were aware of both my experience in ministry and expertise in the financial services arena. I was a consultant to a third party who was the primary spiritual advisor. To date, I am not aware if the Davenports sought the guidance of a financial professional. My lens and contribution to this story were based solely on someone seeking my advice about how to manage this crisis from a spiritual context.

My advice was straightforward. Run, Amy run. My initial observation was that she was incapable of setting boundaries with her family and everyone else dictated her life. She was always bullied into doing things that did not have her best interests at heart. In addition, everyone else in the family was afforded the liberty to live their lives without burdens or sacrifices. If being a woman was the only reason why Amy was selected to care for a mother who had not been the best, then at some point Amy needed to be directly responsible for her mental well-being. Fire and brimstone messages preached from the pulpit were not helpful, and neither were they accurate interpretations of scripture. For example, parents have an obligation toward their children. Scripture does instruct parents accordingly, *"Fathers, do not provoke your children to anger by the way you treat them. Rather, bring them up with the disciple and instruction that comes from the Lord."* (Ephesians 6:4 NLT). One cannot be selective in the interpretation of the Word of God. The other theological argument is simple. It's John's responsibility to love and care for his wife. He must do so as Christ loved the church. He must be willing to give up his life for the mate he selected to journey through life with. If they are truly aligning with scripture and not being selective, then his goal would have been to ensure Amy was married and raising her own family.

But none of that is relevant. This is about a young woman being forced to give up her adulthood to care for a family who did not make the proper emotional investment in her during her formative years growing up. Now, the family wants to benefit from the invisible dividends a sound investment *would* have made if they had heeded scripture accordingly, during a time of need. In the beginning stages, they still had not realized they were suffering a catastrophic loss. They were in the negative as it relates to emotional equity. They had no right to make such a demand on Amy. My advice instructing Amy to run was very intentional and deliberate. Even if she felt the weight of obligation toward the family, if she did not set boundaries at the onset, two or three decades later, she would be destined to potentially live a life of poverty. John had enough life insurance to leave his family capable of maintaining their standard of living, but Rebecca had limited life insurance. As far as the family was concerned, it was not necessary. Her income did not substantially contribute to the economic management of the house. In death, neither the husband's nor wife's transition would diminish the other's quality of life as the years passed. In other words, if John were to die, his insurance would provide for Rebecca and if Rebecca were to die, her income was so limited, it would not contribute to John's overall well-being from day to day.

The Davenports had a healthy investment portfolio that was seriously depleted at the initial stages of Rebecca's illness just with the need to cover the copayment to the Medicare coverage and pick up the gap after those funds were depleted on day 101. It was in their economic best interest to bring Rebecca home for continued care. Their home did not carry a mortgage and property taxes were minimum in

South Carolina. John had done well over the years as a preacher. He was constantly on the road, he was the author of several books, and he was always asked to give a keynote speech for one major social issue or another. He could earn through multiple channels and he had several streams of income. Based on his earnings potential, even if he reduced his schedule, the family could manage the financial costs of a full-time long-term caregiver. A full-time long-term caregiver varied from a live-in nurse. It would require family members to all come together during the off-hours to provide the care Rebecca needed. While John would have been able to continue working, creating an off-hour schedule amongst the seven siblings when he traveled out of town made it possible for him to continue earning at his accustomed rate. He could have limited the impact of potential lost revenue. It would have required him to shift his office hours to include more time at home. It was possible. The average cost in South Carolina was an estimated $5,100 monthly whereas a live-in nurse was almost 50% higher.

Amy, on the other hand, had no guarantee that her family would leave her an inheritance upon her father's death. She did not have a guarantee that anyone would help her financially in any capacity. It was never a consideration. She was in the initial stages of wealth accumulation, and she had not even identified her life purpose. She was in the exploration stages of her life. Here are the questions I presented for consideration after all the ministry jargon was out of the way. The ministry jargon represented scriptures used to manipulate her into submission. I suggested her spiritual advisor give her space and the opportunity to dream. If she could set aside the reality of her present conditions, what would she do with her life? What made her break away and figure out how to survive financially after graduation? I had hoped that if her spiritual counselor could grasp hold of how Amy saw herself, maybe, just maybe she would take the critical next steps. Can you see yourself achieving those goals while taking care of your mother? If you could create a strategic plan to do both, what would it look like?

I gave my opinion since it was solicited. I recommended that Amy provided her family with two options and she needed to stand her ground in what she was proposing. Offer her willingness to facilitate a schedule for everyone in the family to provide round-the-clock care for her mom that would allow her dad to maintain a significant portion of his ministry schedule. She would interview and be responsible for dealing with a reputable long-term caregiver that needed to be hired. But she would not give up her life. She would remain available in the same manner as her siblings and even on her

The Quiet Shift

watch, she would handle some chores around the house. If her first option was outright rebuked or ridiculed, I suggested she pack up and leave. Move far away and begin to pick up the pieces of her life. You may wonder how I can have such extreme suggestions. Based on history, Amy didn't have the strength or esteem to be forceful. If her dad and brothers didn't agree, she would have caved in. That is why her second option would have been to run far away. She would have needed the distance to protect her emotionally and even economically.

When I began writing this book, I considered reaching out to see whatever happened to the Davenports, but I ultimately chose against it. I think I was afraid of the response. As a woman preacher, I have faced criticism from men in different ecumenical circles, yet I have learned to navigate those tumultuous waters. I do hope that the advice I shared was carefully weighed and the family came to a happy medium.

Dear Daddy, It's Me, Jessica

In the healthcare industry, we come across many different people from different backgrounds and stories. Not one case is the same but there are a few that I have come across that stand out, soften my heart, and are truly unforgettable. I will never forget the day Jessica called into my office seeking care for her father Michael who was recently diagnosed with dementia. Jessica had her own family to provide and support and she had no idea how to take care of her father. She also expressed that a nursing home was not an option. My team and I had to collaborate with Michael's doctor's family members in the household and Michael himself to create a care plan to fit his normal routine.

The medical definition for dementia is a disorder caused by damages and or changes to the brain cell's nerves and their connection. In layman's terms, it's a disorder that causes people to forget who they are which can cause someone to act out. It starts subtly, so much so that it may take time for family members to pick up on what is going on. Memory loss, confusing family and friends not recalling who they are, asking a question repeatedly. Michael would cover his tracks effectively during his bouts of being lucid, chalk things up to being tired or having a long day, or even joke about getting old. Then came the struggle to complete a comprehensive thought. Jessica would ask her dad what he was trying to say. She wasn't accustomed to her father not knowing something. After all, he was always smart and very thoughtful, successful in his career. The reality that she could see him withering away was inconceivable. Where was her dad?

The Quiet Shift

As anyone could imagine this was very hard for Jessica to see her father who was her protector, teacher, and provider in this state of mind. When we met Michael in his right state of mind, he was a sweet kindhearted individual who truly has good sense. When he was not lucid, he became mean, loud, aggressive, and angry. This is another symptom of dementia. When someone turns moody, it can be starkly different in demeanor or presence. Michael was not known to be violent or angry, or even depressed. Yet now a regular occurrence would include him throwing things at people when he was upset. He demanded to be pushed around the house in his wheelchair and he even called the police on numerous occasions claiming there were strangers in his home. It was actually a family member who resided with him for his protection. In medical terms, this is known as the sundowning effect.

In Michael's case, as part of our care plan, we sent a nurse to his home to provide 24-hour care. In which the nurse aided with his daily needs as known as ADL's. In short, ADL stands for activities of daily living. Generally, to define what long-term care is, it is the ability to manage one's basic needs in six crucial areas. These areas include bathing, dressing, continence, toileting, transferring or ambulating, and eating. In other words, one must know how to groom themselves, go to the bathroom independently and not lose control of their bladder and bowel function, get dressed, eat and move about without guidance or assistance. Jessica realized she was unable to manage Michael without guidance. So, when the nurse was hired, she was hired to also provide comfort and be a friend, a go-to person when Michael had his moments. Gradually over time, Michael would not be having episodes anymore, he would lose his good sense altogether. Which is truly sad.

The Quiet Shift

Jessica realized there would be value in having an ally with experience addressing individuals destined to deteriorate mentally. In addition, the nurse would be equipped to provide Jessica with insider intel that allowed her to have different, yet direct conversations with her dad. It didn't always make things easier because confrontation can oftentimes be off-putting. Add to that, parents can be quick to remind their children who they are.

I do believe one of the most devastating realities that occur in the parent/child dynamics is the fundamental truth that the roles will eventually change. Parents have the responsibility to raise their children and it is my perspective that even if the full 18 years that society gives the parents that authority, the nature of that relationship shapes and defines how a parent will be treated by their child/children once the parent advances in age. In other words, a parent makes an investment of 18 years, and they will either reap a harvest of great relationships and care when they become older or they will find that their investment into their child when given the opportunity during their baby's most formative years was not substantive enough to ensure their child does not resent the changing of the guard, responsibility to care for the aging parent. A sickness like dementia can test the pressure points in a family relationship.

At first, Jessica didn't realize the hidden costs associated with caring for her father. She didn't understand that he could unlock doors, get in his car, and get lost trying to find his way back. She couldn't comprehend that the father who had always been strong and a leader would leave the stove on and potentially set the house on fire. Or leave his car running or the keys in the door. She needed a babysitter for her dad. The burden was too great, the risk of dad hurting himself too real and she was at her wit's end. Financially this kind of care in the home or facility can become very costly. There are about ten million new cases of dementia every year. Put this way about ten in every 100,000 individuals are diagnosed with onset dementia before the age of sixty-five every year. If you think about it that's a lot of people and most of those people are not financially prepared for this sort of thing. The impact can be devastating because of the nature of care critical to watching someone around the clock.

Let's go back to the natural inclination of people who are enduring this deterioration of the mind. Michael, as with other patients, became quite adept in covering his tracks when he realized during his times of lucidity, he was clear when he messed up and made every effort to cover his tracks. This behavior makes things even more challenging to address when a caregiver doesn't have the full picture of exactly what is taking place with an impacted loved one. In Jessica's case, Michael's understandable deception caused greater anxiety and more importantly, time trying to take corrective action. She was being stretched so thin that it was beginning to impact her spouse and children. I know the reality is difficult to comprehend, but the truth is that everyone goes into survival mode and is on the defensive. Jessica felt terrible because she felt every decision, she made was the wrong decision. She had to tell her dad no constantly and chasten him primarily out of fear that he would cause self-harm. And she was still dealing with the realization that her dad who always appeared invincible, always had the right answers to all her problems, always available to protect her well, was gone, and he would never return. The only comfort she had was that he was so responsible, she didn't have to endure the economic brunt that can cause the elderly to live in poverty at the most vulnerable stages of their life.

Dementia is the most expensive of quality care for an aging senior and it is also one that impacts the average household. It cannot be ignored. When a person's mind begins to deteriorate, it doesn't necessarily impact the body. Therefore, an individual can remain physically healthy and mentally deteriorate simultaneously. That can prolong eventual death and impact someone's overall financial well-being. Michael was successful in his vocation. He retired with a comfortable net worth that included over $1,200,000 in investable assets. He did not have long-term care insurance, something that would impact his estate plan negatively since he was forced to pay for his overall care out of pocket. However, he had enough resources to manage his illness, even if it meant Jessica's inheritance would be reduced somewhat. According to several notable tracking agencies, they average the cost for his level of care to be an estimated $52,000 annually. The care plan the family selected was for Michael to stay home since a skilled nursing care facility was not an option. He would have a full-time aide giving the family the ability to offer around-the-clock care 24/7. This figure does not include the unpaid costs that Jessica endured which were in alignment with the additional, invisible costs of $30,000 each year.

Michael had the necessary resources to address his dementia with a level of dignity and respect. In addition to having money, he had a strong family network. His plan included a loving daughter, a family member active in his overall well-being who lived in the house, and the ability to retain a full-time nurse on staff. His comprehensive financial planning over the years provided him with options, even if he did not have long-term care insurance. The ability to pay out of pocket isn't a viable option for most families. So, what can an average family do financially should they face the reality that their parent has dementia, and they can no longer be trusted to live independently?

Here is an acceptable model for a family to determine economically what they must do to protect themselves from high healthcare costs as they grow older. Let me begin by stating you are never too young to sit with a financial planner to map out your future. The earlier you become aware of potential vulnerabilities that come along with aging, the more protection mechanisms can be implanted to ensure that your goal to accumulate wealth and maintain a decent standard of living is preserved, and whenever possible, the transfer of any remaining net worth is appropriately distributed to the next generation. Advice varies regarding long-term care insurance specifically, but if someone sees they are positioned to have accumulated assets above $500,000, it becomes a very necessary conversation to have. Taking an actual monetary goal out of the equation, here is a simple model to follow. If you have been saving in your retirement plan since you began working and you are investing the minimum amount to get the company to match, then your investment style sets you up to accumulate some level of wealth. Even tracking the S&P 500 over a 35-40-year period while you are working helps you to have a decent retirement pool, provided you do not consistently withdraw money prematurely. Now if you add the purchase of a home to the equation, your overall net worth should be evaluated and ultimately protected.

The Quiet Shift

It is the discipline you show at an early age that makes you more conscious you have an opportunity to become financially free. The sooner the better. Long-term care insurance can become quite costly, but the risk of doing nothing is too expensive of a cost for a family to manage. Today there are too many options available to minimize the risk and we really must do better getting the word out. Statistically speaking, if you and a spouse reach the age of retirement together, at least one of you will have a long-term care need. By that time, it will be too late to make informed decisions. Your options will be dictated by your finances.

Role Reversals

In 2004 I had two similar situations happen within days of each other and I can vividly recall telling each primary caregiver that I was going to write about their lives one day as their needs were similar, but the plan of action impacted them drastically differently. So, with each of their permission, I am sharing the benefit of meeting with an advisor to address the need to have a long-term care strategy, even when it is too late to purchase long-term care insurance. In addition, details have changed to protect their privacy overall. What made them stand out? Imagine a client walking into your office needing guidance because their elderly parent just sold their home because they recognize it was too dangerous to live alone. Now they have a pool of resources, yet they are displaced, advanced in age, and are being forced to adapt to a new environment.

When Angel came into my office, she was extremely clear. We clicked immediately because she was upfront about her objectives and honestly, she made me laugh. She hands me a check of approximately $375,000 and these instructions, "I just sold my mom's house, and I am putting her in a nursing home. I need you to make sure she never has to live with me. I don't care if there isn't a penny left." Her mom, Ms. Grant, was advanced in age and a chain smoker. The prospective client Angel was in her early 70s, married, and financially stable. She was granted power of attorney and wanted to make her mom as comfortable as possible for her final years on earth. After engaging in further conversation, I knew I could put together a strategic plan that would meet both her mom's and her objectives.

In 2004, the Medicaid look-back period was three years and because of the Deficit Reduction Act of 2005 was poised to change the rules drastically for Long Term Care Medicaid eligibility. In short, as of February 2006, the look-back period would increase from 36 months to 60 months. For an individual to qualify for Medicaid, their assets needed to be accounted for. In other words, one could not simply give their money away and still qualify for Medicaid. If money was drawn down or given away, it was still used to calculate if one qualified for medical financial support.

Angel's mother was still relatively independent, so we opted to research long-term care facilities that provided assisted living and skilled nursing care. While the goal was for mom to never move into Angel's house, she still wanted her mom to have comfort and stability. Moving from site to site as her mom's health deteriorated was illogical and avoidable. There was no long-term care insurance and mom did not have substantial savings outside of the sale of her home. Her monthly income was modest, so she didn't have the challenges that New Jersey presented as an income cap state. That means New Jersey residents oftentimes are not qualified for Medicaid if their annual income exceeds a certain threshold. If one's income is higher, the amount of assets becomes immaterial since the patient would be disqualified to receive benefits.

With the lump sum of money, coupled with the modest monthly income being brought in, I suggested the mom make a substantial lifetime gift to Angel. At that stage, Angel already had complete control of her mom's finances and had been managing them with integrity for years. The probability of her taking her mom's money and running away appeared minimal. We had the mom's full assurance, she felt comfortable with the suggestion. We transferred $250,000 into Angel's name and left the remaining $125,000 in the mom's name. We found a long-term care facility that offered a semi-private room from independent living to assisted living to the ultimate nursing home. The estimated costs were just shy of $40,000 leaving money for basic needs and care essentials, including the mom's very expensive cigarette habit that remained until the day she took her last breath. The remaining money was used to self-pay for the long-term care facility selected. It included all meals, senior activities, and medical assistance on-site. Ms. Grant was able to manage the risk for three years, making her eligible for Medicaid, which she applied for after 3 ½ years. She had no problems applying and lived in that facility for an additional 4 years without any complications. Angel subsidized her monthly expenses and paid to keep her mom in a semi-private room. It was an additional monthly cost of $750.

The money gifted to Angel was invested wisely with a balanced investment strategy. We opted for that course of action for two reasons. First, longevity was inherent, and second, while Angel was financially stable, she did not have long-term care insurance either. Taking care of her mom made her realize the strategy we were implementing for her mom would not work for her. Between her and her husband, their combined income substantially exceeded the income cap amount. Medicaid was not an option for her. So, when the risk was virtually eliminated at the beginning of year 3, we met with designated Medicaid representatives and were assured Ms. Grant would have no issues. Angel then decided to incrementally support her grandson by establishing a 529 Plan. The original $250,000 had grown modestly and we determined that we would use the remaining assets as the pool of resources allocated to their long-term care needs. Because Angel had four successful, financially independent children devoted to their parents, home care was the most logical for them. The goal was to have the remaining pool of resources available or targeted for their care. Seventeen years later, the money is still growing and has grown since 2008 when the strategy was shifted from balance to growth. In 2020, we reduced the investment risk back to balance when Angel moved closer to 90 years of age.

Both Angel and Jim, her husband, remain in their primary residence and the goal remains the same. They are both in their 90s and when the time arises, they have enough resources for home care. In addition to the resources, they have made arrangements with their children to have an outside agency provide the necessary support to complement the children's availability. The children are not only capable but willing, to pay out of pocket any supplemental costs as their parents' needs increase over time. This is a primary example of an entire family coming together to create a strategic plan to invest, manage and ultimately leave wealth to the next generation. Ms. Grant did not have a strategy, but Angel was wise enough to seek out the services of a financial planner. Realizing that she was also vulnerable and too old to purchase long-term care, they did not ignore the potential financial tsunami that could have impacted their comfortable standard of living, they made the necessary adjustments. The investment into their grandson was to ensure wealth would not die two generations removed.

The Quiet Shift

In addition to the steps they took, each of their children purchased long-term care insurance so that losing their overall net worth to a critical illness would not be a part of their legacy. Provided they all continue to work with a financial planner, it is now standard practice in their family. The family has successfully managed to protect their generational wealth and it was based on a decision to meet with a professional capable of helping them navigate through a potentially financially devasting medical concern.

The second family was similar in that Jenny's parents had just sold their home and they were reluctantly moving into the same house with Jenny. Mr. Carrington had recently retired and his wife, Mrs. Carrington stayed home and raised the children and it was never necessary for her to gain employment. They lived an extremely comfortable lifestyle, managed to save a healthy nest egg, and accumulated over a million dollars in assets, not including the profit from the sale of the house which added $300,000 to overall resources. They were averse to risk and walked into the bank hell-bent on placing the proceeds from the sale of the house in FDIC-insured products. Someone recommended they "have a conversation" with a financial planner.

After sitting with the family for a short period, I requested their permission to ask targeted questions that were less about investing their money and more about the quality of life they desired to have in the twilight season of their lives. This was very important because Mr. Carrington worked hard to provide for the family. And one must recognize there is security in receiving a steady paycheck. Because they were moving in with their daughter, I wanted to know what their expectations of her were. They hadn't considered her in the equation. Her life was drastically altered as well. She was self-employed and due to multiple unanticipated medical issues, that arose at the most inopportune times, she was forced to scale back her business plans and the way she was operating at the time. I thought it was important to paint a vivid picture from the lens of a daughter who was taking on the permanent responsibility of becoming the primary caregiver to parents while simultaneously raising her children and managing her marriage. Several things I wanted them to consider were the economic impact, the management of time, and the potential for burnout given Jenny had young children.

When a family decides to manage in-home long-term care with a family member as the primary caregiver, the expenses decrease drastically. Statistically speaking, most of the care at home is provided by unpaid caregivers which tend to be women more than men. Going in these directions, the average cost of services which can range from $200-$350 each day can truly add up. While there is an immediate direct saving, the next generation of beneficiaries is deeply impacted. In other words, Jenny's ability to accumulate wealth is stifled. Realizing time was on my side and the resources were available, I made a bold recommendation. Mr. Carrington, "I want you and Mrs. Carrington to consider gifting Jenny $250,000 each for a total of $500,000." The money would have represented approximately 40% of their overall estate. Why did I think that was critical? While Mr. and Mrs. Carrington had enough resources to self-pay for critical care, it would deplete assets over time and Jenny was losing out on earnings potential and the possible inheritance. Since there would be a three-year lookback for Medicaid eligibility, setting aside money for

Jenny's future was mentally and economically essential. She had a family, goals, and dreams that were being set aside to provide for her parents.

The elderly Carrington's balked, and Jenny sat in silence, shocked. I calmly explained my "why" and I had two primary reasons. The first was the lost earnings that Jenny would suffer undertaking the responsibility. I asked them to consider their grandchildren, their needs, and their futures. Surely, as grandparents they want their grandchildren to have a chance to go to college and not be overwhelmed by debt. I suggested that Jenny and her husband may need a house more ideal for two aging parents, that perhaps to best accommodate them, the logistics of their current environment may no longer be sufficient. What it all boiled down to was that generationally speaking, with the resources Jenny could invest wisely with a growth strategy so that her dreams or family objectives would remain possible. Since Mr. Carrington had always relied upon FDIC-insured products, asking him to invest to offset any potential risks associated with the diminished purchasing power of a dollar over time would have been a losing battle. The second reason was equally important. If one parent became chronically ill for an extended period, the family could technically spend down on their assets due to the mounting medical costs associated with an extended illness. What would happen to the surviving spouse? If that unknown variable was unaddressed, it could be problematic. One thing not being considered in the move was the fact that spouses tend to provide for each other until the responsibilities become too overwhelming for the healthier party. The Carringtons were bypassing that norm and moving right in with Jenny. Her proximity would be automatically hindering.

That needed to be included in the overall discussion.

To my pleasant surprise, we compromised. Honestly, I decided to aim high with the hope that we could settle in a space of a lifetime gift that was manageable. Jenny's parents understood she would be the ultimate final beneficiary of the residual estate and that she was undertaking a major responsibility for which they were grateful. Yet shifting a half million dollars was a tall ask. The number we landed on was $300,000 and the seniors still retained control of their assets, which was more than a million dollars. Within the year, Mr. Carrington's health declined rapidly and after dealing with an elevated chronic illness, hospital visits multiple times a week, and the constant barrage of doctors, doctors, and more doctors, Mr. Carrington transitioned peacefully within the first year of our business relationship. While the purpose of sharing this story is primarily regarding the impact of long-term care or lack thereof, we did complete a comprehensive estate plan to minimize tax liability on the second death of the elderly Carrington. In other words, their estate planning included leveling the assets so that the second to die would not trigger a huge estate tax liability. The federal estate tax exemption at that time was 1.5MM, but there is no tax liability when the spouse is the beneficiary. If an estate can surpass the exemption amount, a wise practice is to include a contingency for that possibility.

We were aware of the need because we had completed a comprehensive financial plan, which includes additional assets that are not limited to but include life insurance. Ms. Carrrington was set for life. Any anxiety about gifting Jenny dissipated once she realized she was in a great financial position and would never lack anything she desired for the remainder of her life. Incidentally, Ms. Carrington lived an additional 15 years. For the first dozen, she was fiercely independent and enjoyed the role of great grandma. She liked to travel, and she made certain holidays a really big deal. She also contributed generously to her local church and worthy causes that served to be economically beneficial from a tax perspective.

It was Jenny who faced challenges once the money was gifted to her. At the time of the original gift, she was married for more than 25 years and counting. While I advised her not to commingle the money into a joint account, slowly over time, some funds were commingled in the interest of the family deciding to purchase a new house out of the state of New Jersey. When someone receives a living inheritance, it is treated in the same manner as an inheritance at death. The beneficiary does not have to share it with their spouse, provided they keep the assets separate. Fortunately, I had earned the trust of the family enough that when I offered a best practice strategy for Jenny's windfall of money, she took my advice. This can be a very difficult conversation to have when you have been in a committed relationship for such a long time. In addition, one must tread carefully. It's very difficult to bring up a "what if" case scenario, especially when there are little or no signs of marital angst.

In this case, I had the support of Mr. Carrington who was a very principled individual. I simply explained in detail the consequences of gifting money. You relinquish control, you have no say in how the beneficiary spends the money and you cannot request the money back. One might ask why wasn't trust a consideration. Simply put, while trusts are ideal tools, this family's dynamics were slightly different. Jenny needed some economic autonomy. However, Mr. Carrington expressly understood he would have no influence over the control of the assets and insisted at least they remain in Jenny's name only. Fortunately, she listened because shortly after his death, as previously stated, the family purchased a new house and car. Mr. Carrington's death added money to her inheritance. Jenny's family sold their primary house, purchased a larger residence in another state, and added money into the house to reduce the monthly mortgage payment. The new home was in the name of Jenny and her spouse. When there was trouble in paradise, the unimaginable became a reality. She was headed to divorce court and the largest asset Jenny owned had been commingled with her husband making it a marital asset that was subjected to the 50/50 dissolution. She could buy him out, he could buy her out, or they could sell the house and split the proceeds.

How did Jenny take a loss in the scenario? In addition to rolling over the proceeds from the sale of the first property, Jenny added $100,000 to the purchase of the new house. It wasn't the original gift. She received it after her dad's death. Immediately, she would take a financial hit because only 50% of that additional investment was able to be recovered. Secondly, Jenny was in a better financial position to keep the new house they just purchased in a new state. She had small children to consider and a mother with whom she was the primary caregiver. Transitioning to a new environment was exhausting standing alone. What would be the best course of action, both financially and emotionally? One additional barrier remained present. Before Jenny became a primary caregiver to her parents, she was self-employed oftentimes showing a loss in her business. Refinancing in her name individually was challenging, but we managed to limit her financial loss in the divorce to the contribution made initially. She had to transfer more of her inheritance into the house once she became the sole owner and she relinquished the family car as a part of the settlement. If we had not kept the original gift segregated, the financial pain would have been greater.

Things did not improve because Jenny did not qualify for long-term care insurance. The primary reason why she became an entrepreneur was lingering health challenges that would rear their ugly head at the most inopportune time. In addition, the medical insurance she did have was through her husband's employer. In the divorce settlement, it was negotiated she would remain covered for an additional three years. Just when the coverage was set to be terminated, she met and married a wonderful man who provided emotional and medical support. Together they cared for Mrs. Carrington who lived well into her nineties before eventually transitioning. Throughout the years, the financial plan included giving Jenny an annual gift up to the maximum amount.

The goal was to ensure all parties, Mr. and Mrs. Carrington, along with their daughter Jenny, would have quality care and the necessary medical treatment as everyone grew old. They understood the challenges and they came up with a financial strategy that considered everyone's life. Would it have been ideal and more cost-efficient if they had met with a planner much earlier? Absolutely. However, because they had economic means, they were still able to minimize the overall cost typically associated with caring for an aging parent. In

The Quiet Shift

this case, the assets were preserved, and the inheritance was passed on to Jenny. Today Jenny remains happily married and her financial plan has taken into consideration her desire to leave an inheritance to both her children and grandchildren.

Simpson & Stanford

To Thine Own Self be Kind

The most devastating cases long-term care professionals encounter is with people we have an existing relationship with, close or distant. I can recall when I first opened my practice Stanford Angels, LLC. I ran into an old friend whom I was excited to spend time with and catch up on life. We met in school and were such great friends that it was not unusual for me to be at Rachel's house or Rachel at mine for dinner or just a basic sleepover. I knew her family well and she knew mine. There was a time when we were so close that Debbie, her mom, was like a second mom to me and I would address her as such. Rachel embraced my family as well. During our time together, I simply asked her how Debbie was and as Rachel began to talk about her mom, the tears welled up in her eyes. It felt as if all the anxiety, frustration, and fear of losing her mom which was bottled up, came barreling out with permission. She had the opportunity to release her feelings describing what life felt like as a child watching their mom die a slow and painful death. It was surreal because, for a moment, I felt that she had crawled into an emotional child-like cocoon and spoke as a little girl. Rachel felt helpless and hopeless, angry, and afraid. She was angry that her mom didn't take care of her, that she was derelict and now Rachel was suffering because of her mom's poor decisions.

The truth is that Debbie was a woman who never practiced self-care. She was sick and much of the pain she endured was self-inflicted. Unfortunately, it is the life resume of many black women who manage pain as a badge of honor. The truth is that pain is a signal that something is wrong. Black women have been taught to endure the pain and keep pressing forward. Until when? Many make attempts to course correct when it's too late. This was exactly what Debbie was facing. She never took care of herself and as Rachel was recalling the story, she couldn't even pinpoint a date when her mom has ever gone to the doctor. So, when her mom had taken ill to the point that an ambulance needed to be called, they were not prepared for the diagnosis that awaited their arrival. Her mom had been diagnosed with chronic kidney disease. To make matters worse, it had already metastasized and since it was stage 4, all treatment options were no longer viable. To get to stage four, Debbie had to ignore the weight loss and poor appetite. She dismissed the blood that may have shown up in her urine or the constant urge to pee, especially at night. She had to think that being continually exhausted or haven swollen ankles, feet, and hands were natural symptoms associated with getting old. Maybe the inability to sleep, insomnia, or the feeling sick with headaches or itchy skin should have been a clue. But no, Debbie and many others, ignored the signs because they were deemed "incidental" or "not a big deal" until they were lumped together and now, she is facing death because during it all, at stage four of this diagnosis, getting a kidney transplant was out of the question.

How does one accept pain without inquiring about its source? Why would any individual suffer unnecessarily without trying to determine the root of the issue? When something like this occurs, typically the entire family must face the reality that their loved family member was going to die, and they would die much sooner than anyone had time to prepare for emotionally. Let's think about it for a moment. As a child, we do not see our parents as humans who may be frail and mere mortals. We think mommy and daddy can do anything, they are invincible, untouchable. The first time a child catches wind that their parents are sick in any manner, it's a shock to the system. It is a negative, vicious cycle that must be broken. We must begin to listen to our bodies while taking into consideration that our lives have value. For most people, there is someone who loves you enough that they will be devastated when you are no longer on this earth, especially if you are a parent. Is it easier when you have other family members to share your grief with? Absolutely. The burden of caregiving can then be shared and that is always helpful.

At the same time, what if a chronically ill person doesn't have a family? Or maybe the person taken ill has one child. The pressures and responsibilities are greater when it's left to one child to manage. This was Rachel's plight. She was an only child who had not even six years earlier dealt with the loss of her father. His death was a bit easier to deal with because she had her mom by her side. But now, Rachel, who represents children of all races, cultures, and social and economic statuses, must deal with trying to care for a mother while processing that her mom will not live to see memories not yet experienced.

In addition, Rachel becomes the front line of defense. She represents every child who managed to maintain some type of relationship with their parent, consensual or coercive. She is the face of what a family looks like when the tables are turned. Think about it for a moment. Your parents invest in you at the beginning stages of your life. The truth is that based on that initial investment for the first cycle of your life, will define the dynamics of your relationship with your parents for the next 2-3 generations. In simple math, a parent can impart wisdom, guidance, and instruction to their children for the first 20 years of their life, and based on the success or failure rate, the children will engage with their parents for the

The Quiet Shift

next 40-60 years in accordance. If the impartation was healthy, life becomes more manageable for all parties involved. Unfortunately, everyone does not have the most ideal relationship with their parents. Yet the burden or obligation or pressure to step up and care for a parent is always present.

So, my heart broke just a little bit as I attempted to comfort Rachel while she was attempting to stand strong for her mom. There was no one else. I expressed that I was available to help, support, and guide the family as they made this devastating transition. My goal was to first make Debbie comfortable, and secondly, try to guide Rachel through the many devastating, difficult decisions she would be forced to make in the upcoming weeks or months ahead, depending upon how long her mom lived. I recall making an appointment to visit the house the following day. As I walked through the door, my eyes were immediately fixated on Debbie, sitting in the living room with her face speaking volumes. She was wrecked with pain and her visible discomfort made me somewhat uncomfortable because this was "mom", someone I know. To make matters more complicated, I felt as if I let the family down. You may be wondering how and why? Simply put, when we know better, we need to both do better and teach others to do what we know is best for them.

I do know that healthcare management is not only critical to the health and welfare of families, but I also know that if it isn't implemented, it can serve as an impediment to a family. It is a primary reason why families cannot advance economically out of poverty. The truth is that there was very little I could offer the family. Because the sickness was so advanced, the writing was on the wall. The question was simply how long Debbie would remain in pain. During the first three months of compassionate care, we made every attempt to transfer the correct verbiage for Rachel to give to the primary care physician simply to address pain management in some capacity. Debbie was in excruciating pain. She was always cold with trembling legs that remained swollen. Her feet were constantly sore to the touch. She could not breathe easily, and her blood pressure remained extremely high.

To add to the stress, I felt a great deal of empathy for Rachel because she was making every effort to manage her mother's emotions while facing the reality that she had mere months, perhaps days left with the woman who birthed her. Debbie didn't make it easy. She was not the easiest patient to deal with, lashing out at the support circle because she was in pain. Words hurt and at a time when bonding and creating final memories were most critical for Rachel's emotional well-being, Debbie did not make great efforts to consider her daughter's emotions. As an only child, for Rachel, Debbie was the second parent she was forced to bury. Our team did everything possible to make a bad situation better, but our hands were tied.

I didn't know when, but I braced myself knowing that the call would eventually come in. In May 2020, while my nurse was at the house, an ambulance needed to be called and Debbie was rushed to the hospital. We were approximately four months into services, just offering support for a few hours weekly on an as-needed basis because Debbie did not have a long-term care strategy at all. At the same time, Covid-19 was looming over the country in a major way so hospice care had to be in home confinement. The moment her mom went into the hospital, Rachel was not even permitted to see her mother again. Mere days later, that call came in and Debbie was dead. Anyone who experienced death after March 2020 and for the remainder

The Quiet Shift

of the year, had added complications with making final arrangements for a loved one. Funerals were out of the question, so Rachel suffered alone, literally.

There was no good outcome for Rachel. Sickness unfortunately is a way of life. Having said that, we are all given one body and it is our responsibility to be good stewards accordingly. Some things are truly preventable. If there is a message I can share with the world, it is that I implore you to visit the doctors regularly. Even if you choose to not take the prevention route, when your body gives you signals, listen to them. Maybe if Debbie had made a practice of visiting the doctor more often, her diagnosis would have been discovered at an earlier stage providing her with more options. To die in America at just over 60 years old is tragic indeed. I just believe it's too young to be gone. An annual physical can go a long way. Your health comes first.

My Children Are My Retirement Plan

I know a mother who raised four beautiful daughters and she would continually remind them that they were her retirement and long-term care plans. She explicitly stated that she was investing in them and that if she did her job correctly, they would provide for her in her later years. She took a calculated risk banking on the fact that out of four daughters, at least two of them would prove her right. It sounds good, but is it right? All adults should process what I am saying right now. Ask yourself a few questions. Do you want your son or your daughter to change you, bathe you, and make sure you have a roof over your head or clothes on your back when you have always been accustomed to taking care of them? Do you desire for them to give up on their hopes and dreams and life goals to take care of you? Are you concerned about their children and your child's inability to choose to show up for their children who may be actively engaged in recreational activities or take you to the doctor? Furthermore, did your children ask to be born, and do you honestly feel like they owe you for their lives that they had no control over?

I know these questions may appear harsh, but they are real. The woman who made that declaration calculation paid off. I am the second eldest of four girls, with my eldest sister being almost three years my senior and the baby being ten years my junior. My younger sister is approximately fourteen months younger, and we are extremely close. There were several desires/mandates/principles our mom drilled into our heads that have guided us all. The first mandate was that we would all graduate from college. She believed education was the greatest weapon to level the playing field for anyone who desired success in their lives. The second desire was that we would be friends and love each other unconditionally. She believed that there was no one else we should ever need to count on since we had each other. She died freely believing her desire was fulfilled. It's the final mandate that initially appeared glib, but something she meant wholeheartedly. She expected her children to provide for her in retirement and when she grew old.

Let me explain the dynamics of my relationship with my mom. It was not always a healthy relationship. However, during her later years in life, we managed to accept the challenges of our past and we began to bond in a substantial, meaningful way. I believe she died very proud of all her children and what we managed to accomplish. I also believe she was gone too soon, and her death could have been preventable. Our relationship was the most turbulent of the four daughters so whenever she said we were her retirement and long-term care plan, my sisters and I would entertain what we perceived to be her folly. The breakdown went something like this, she would live with my oldest and baby sister. I would write the check for her care and my stair stepsister would be the bridge between everyone. Settled. I am number four. In other words, I would be the last person responsible for my mother's day-to-day care. I am the fourth or the final option. It was with the hopes that we would never get to me because my mom would grow old and die in her sleep. Isn't that what most people plan for?

Without going into detail, Wilma had a routine medical procedure that landed her in ICU and that was the first time we considered the mortality of mommy. I honestly believe kids grow up believing their parents are invincible. That was the beginning of her health deteriorating slowly. She eventually stopped working and lived in subsidized housing with a retirement disability income. She did not lack anything and whatever Wilma wanted, her daughters came through. So, when she wanted to go see Denzel Washington in The Equalizer and have dinner at BBQs in New York for her birthday in September of 2014, we were there although the baby did not join us on that excursion. It was the first time we all noticed she didn't eat much food. It led to a conversation called, "How long have you not been eating?" She downplayed the seriousness of what she was feeling. The conversation did not end there. As sisters, we attempted to piece together what we knew about Wilma medically. I confess I was somewhat out of the loop because my siblings lived in the same city, and I was well over 40 minutes away. They all shared a major bond with my mother that I cannot say that I had. If we had a universal regret, it would probably be that we didn't move with a greater sense of urgency.

On Thursday, October 30th, 2014, Wilma was taken to the emergency room and admitted into the hospital. Initially, we took it lightly because, well, that was Wilma. We were planning a surprise birthday party for my oldest sister who was born on Halloween. She had been out of the country for so long, we were going to celebrate her 45th birthday. Wilma had a way of making sure she always remained the center of attention, so a hospital stay took the cake. She insisted we went ahead with the plans with no one thinking it was anything serious. The medical doctors simply wanted to run a few tests and that was that. The first sign of trouble was when the doctors appeared indecisive about what was going on and the attempts to complete a simple gastroscopy were failing. A gastroscopy is a test that lowers a camera down your throat to view your throat, the esophagus, and your stomach. The test made sense to us because she was having trouble eating food. They moved her from a regional hospital to a trauma center better equipped to find the root of her pain. At the second hospital, it was test after test for at least another four to five days before the doctors would even identify the issue. Stage four pancreatic cancer that had already metastasized was the eventual verdict. We were stunned!

Questions were running through everyone's mind. What happened? How did this happen? What does it mean? Do we tell the children? You see, the moment we found out the diagnosis, we all ran to google to see what Wilma's options were. We learned the sobering news that it was one of the most devastating cancers with a shortened life expectancy of one year after a typical diagnosis. We found out that her treatment options were extremely limited, and they would not necessarily add years to her life, months if she were fortunate. Just in the journey of discovery, it was a full two weeks before the possibility of Wilma being released from the hospital ever came up. We had no clue about the real impact, and we had to face the reality that Wilma was going to die, and she was going to die sooner than any of us were ever prepared for. I couldn't afford to react because everything was happening at such a dizzying pace that processing emotions was simply not an option. You see, my being #4 went right out the window. At this moment, Wilma's long-term care plan had to go into full effect, and it looked nothing like we all joked about for the many years before this new reality.

What were the circumstances in our lives that dictated our actions? That's a story for my siblings to share from their perspective but broadly speaking, this is what we were dealing with. Nita and T lived with Mommy, and they

The Quiet Shift

shared three sons among them. Mommy's house was not the most ideal living quarters because the bedrooms were designed to be separated from the community space. In other words, to be among everyone, she would have had to contend with a staircase and three young men running around. At the same time, Nita gets hit by a car and she needed to recover. Sonji had serious medical issues. She was fighting the issues so much that I thought at one point I would have two people living as roommates in the makeshift hospital room we were preparing for Mommy. To make matters worse, Wilma coming to live with me was never a part of the conversation. Remember, I was always #4. Can we just be honest? Wilma dreaded coming to live with me as well. She would have picked any other place, insisted she was going home and as I have been for most of our lives, I stepped up to be the bad guy. As soon as Wilma was hospitalized, we sat as a family and quickly put together a simple will, health care proxy, and durable power of attorney. It was the benefit of my expertise. I was designated the agent to make the decisions while she was alive and the executor upon her eventual death. Wilma had a metal box that she used to always say, "*This is my box of problems. Give it to Nikki when I'm gone.*"

Finally, I firmly decided that my house made the most sense and everybody please just get on board. Fortunately, everyone lined up with it. My family could create the schedule most suitable to ensure that someone was always with Mommy. We had the space with a bathroom right across the hall from a spacious bedroom. The kitchen and living room were steps away from the bedroom so she wouldn't suffer in isolation. It was ideal for everyone… except me. My house was a toxic environment for me during that time, and I was preparing to move

The Quiet Shift

out. I had been recently divorced and we were all still living under the same roof. I needed to be the disruptor once again with the declaration that I was now staying AND my momma is moving in... period. Thank God my ex-husband is a decent individual. I would have never survived without his support and assistance. While we may not have been great together, he was always an amazing father and a beloved son-in-law. He took care of my mom with unconditional love and no bitterness about us. I will always appreciate his sacrifice.

Wilma was not given a choice. I had never considered being a primary caregiver and I am most certain she was not happy about moving in with me. I know this because she told me. In one of our many conversations during that season, she shared that she thought I was going to beat her upside the head with Jesus' rhetoric. I laughed so hard because that is NOT how the

Simpsons roll. Here is the other critical thing. After deciding where Wilma would reside, we had to address what level of care she would pursue. As sisters, of course, we all wanted her to fight, fight, fight. But Wilma said something at the hospital that made me take on a different perspective. It took the hospital approximately two weeks before the doctors even articulated she had a chance to go home. She had been resigned to the fact she was going to die, and she verbalized that she was okay. She told us that her life was tremendously blessed and that she was content. If the Lord saw fit to bring her home, she would have lived a wonderful life. Now, if you know where Wilma came from and the trauma she experienced, to hear that gave me pause because things turned out just fine.

In one of our many pow-wows, as siblings we decided to support Wilma in whatever path she chose regarding her life. That was difficult and painful and Wilma made her choice. Yet we understood pragmatically that it boiled down to maintaining a decent quality of life, living her last days comfortably, or going through chemotherapy for a few additional months, not years. Wilma chose to have a decent quality of life and we went about as dutiful daughters, making memories as best we could. It was tough. She didn't want anyone to see her in her declining state, so we angered a lot of family members, even among ourselves. No one could visit her at the hospital, and we were preparing for her release. We were disappointed because we shifted Thanksgiving to my house only to find out she would not be released. We told the grandkids on a need-to-know basis because several were in college, and we didn't want to disrupt their peace. She came to her new home, and we made her as comfortable as possible. This was not the plan.

I don't think people understand the need to have a viable plan of action for aging parents, let alone parents who are enduring an elevated illness. As a society, we must come to grips with death. One thing is certain, we are all born to die, and we must normalize this reality. When Wilma came to 1438 (that's my affectionate name for my house), we settled into a schedule while I made certain provisions to shift my business practices. You see, I was self-employed, the owner of a financial planning firm and in school pursuing my Master of Divinity degree full-time. All of that was changing. I was trying to finish the semester and then put a pause on school. I had just sent out a mass letter to my clients with a change of work hours so that I could go into my office early in the morning and be home for the remainder of the day, available to take mom to the doctor and hospital whenever necessary. Our baby sister T would take care of the boys, Nita would focus on recovering from the car accident, and Sonji would be my relief. If Mommy needed or wanted anything, Sonji would bring it faithfully at least at a minimum on Fridays. That was my allocated break time. My children stepped in and offered comic relief and continual entertainment. Jeseman made certain Wilma wanted nothing and helped make sure we transported Wilma to the doctor appointments she had. While it was not the plan, we settled into a schedule that worked for everyone and appeared to be minimally invasive to all parties... except me.

My life was not supposed to be what it was in 2014. Forget about everyone else for a moment, parents have a responsibility to consider their children as they get older. It isn't fair to assume your children will care for you. I know, the subject is taboo, but we must normalize it, especially if you are a child who experienced pain and suffering growing up. The burden of caregiving is real. I am intentional about sharing with parents and children the importance of allowing a caregiver space to decompress. Their lives are being uprooted and they didn't sign up for the job. In my case, my personal life was in shambles, and I was trying to find myself. Mom's plan didn't include me carrying the weight of caregiving and neither did mine. But when we found out the devastating news, we rallied together because that's what families do. Wilma was correct in this-she made a significant investment in her four daughters, and she expected it to pay dividends when she needed it the most. Wilma lacked or desired nothing. We covered her.

I was most concerned about Wilma transitioning during the holiday season. I did not want any of the grandchildren to be permanently scarred by the first major death that would impact them all. Outside of my niece and my daughter, everyone else had not truly experienced the loss of a loved one. It hurts. But the time she stayed with us was a very necessary season in our lives because I learned afterward that my children felt cheated out of a grandmother. You see, I moved far enough away from home to *preserve* a relationship with my mom. I never considered the impact it would have on my children. Both of my kids had a chance to bond in such a personal way that it was truly a blessing to be capable of being the one to care for her during her final days.

It was important for me to maintain my mother's dignity as well. Both being critically ill and advanced in age may require children to care for their adult parents. They may have to perform the activities of daily living. Bathing a parent, and helping them in the restroom are not easy responsibilities. Yet it must be done and if a parent does not have the financial ability to hire a full-time nurse, a family member will have to step up. Those moments were private. I didn't even allow Jeseman or my children to help me. I still suffer from chronic back pain years later. We were fortunate enough to have compassionate care where a professional stopped by several days a week. She managed most of the bathing... again, to preserve Wilma's dignity.

My family, Wilma's girls, were tremendously blessed. Because she decided to enjoy life for her remaining days, we focused on simply loving her unconditionally and making every desire a reality. I spent more hours in deep conversations learning about my mother in a whole different way. Some deep-rooted painful experiences were addressed, and the sharing of stories created a pathway for healing. Wilma used to always say that parenting didn't come with a blueprint and that she didn't have an instruction manual for us. What I appreciated most was her reflective posture. She could live with me because we had been on a great relational path for at least 10-15 years at that juncture. For me, it was a no-brainer. Scripture tells us to *"Honour thy father and thy mother: that thy days may be long upon the land which the Lord thy God giveth thee."* (Exodus 20:12.) What was still extremely painful at the point of decision, was the reality that she wanted to go anywhere except 1438. Did I understand it? Yes. Did it still sting just a little bit? Yes. Did I get over it? Yes.

After hearing Rachel's story, I knew I had to tell mine. Two African American women who did not practice self-care died prematurely. Wilma was sixty-three years young. My family did not suffer long. We found out at the end of October 2014 and Wilma died peacefully surrounded by all of us on January 9th, 2015. As her four daughters, we wrote her a letter that was shared at her celebration of life. The part that remains forever etched in my heart reads as follows.

It was best for you to spend your last days with Jesse, Nikki, and the kids. They needed to bond with you as the Simpson family. We think you were able to see that she took your advice because she reflects the best of who you are, and she has trusted her instincts and relied upon what was within to navigate through life. You used to say, "Learn from my mistakes and don't repeat them." She was the one who expressed the anger of our youth so clearly, but the first to decide her past would not dictate her future. She was finally able to truly believe you were so very, very proud of her.

I don't know the dynamics of your family history, but what I do know is that we owe it to one another to be considerate of the people we

The Quiet Shift

are connected to. No one else, whether it's by choice or through obligation, will typically step up to care for you during your most vulnerable state. Should you recognize that you haven't operated with a spirit of excellence when rearing your children, today is a great day to reconcile. Debbie and Wilma didn't have a lot of money. They both needed their children in the latter season of their lives. But how they lived mattered. Rachel still has deep-rooted scars because of her mother's treatment. On the other hand, Wilma's girls, while we may have some issues, we were blessed to call her mom. If we had to do it all over again, it would still be our privilege.

Simpson & Stanford

Doing Everything Right

How does one accumulate, maintain, and distribute wealth when one does not have a historical blueprint to review? You begin to learn about what you don't know. When I was in the fourth grade, my teacher arranged a field trip to the New York Stock Exchange. The experience changed my life. I was in awe of the financial services industry and what trading meant. I don't know if I truly grasped its power then, but I walked away recognizing I wanted companies that were flashing on that big screen. Having those letters meant having money. I entered the industry at a very young age because my life veered off the course I thought would take. I fully intended to pursue a basketball career followed by becoming a judge. That is no secret. But I landed where I needed to be and my desire to acquire wealth was no longer abstract. It began to take shape. The first thing I learned was the importance of systematic investments and the best place to begin was in your 401K. I'm going somewhere with what I learned so stay with me. The second thing I learned was that when I saved money, my company would match what I saved up to a certain percentage. I knew I couldn't touch it until I turned 59 ½, but what made me commit to savings was when I realized the relationship between my potential tax and my retirement savings. Studying it in a classroom and watching it unfold hit me differently.

I began to formulate a story. It was hard. I was just over 25 years old working on delivering a message to people that stated to break the generational curse of poverty, we needed to set aside a little bit each pay period. I wanted to let them know the sooner we get started, the better off we would become if we wanted to acquire wealth. I was experiencing the potential truth in

The Quiet Shift

my own life. When I had been in the industry for almost a decade, in 1999, I decided it was time. I would focus on building my own book of business simultaneously while working with a team. Managing wealthy people's money was not the issue and my advice was not on the line. I was the junior associate. It takes on a different level of pressure when the buck stops with you. Dana believed me. She is five years my junior and I met her just before I turned 30 years old. She didn't want to work all her life and had nothing to show for it, not at retirement, but when she hit 40 years old. She wanted to live "comfortably". She was one of my first personal clients outside of the team I had been working with and she was willing to follow my advice. I had just finished the journey of becoming a CFP® practitioner.

Creating strategies to accumulate wealth comes easily to me. It's staying on track to achieve your goals when life gets in the way that makes things much more complicated. I knew wealth accumulation was necessary, but after being directly impacted by the tragedy of September 11, 2001, I recognized protection was equally important. I mean the protection of life, protection of the ability to earn, and protection from health challenges that can arise and thwart the best laid-out plan. What most people don't realize or consider is what I experienced personally at the tender age of 30. Had I not been in the World Trade Center and experienced the trauma firsthand, I would not have been a major advocate for disability or life insurance. It was dealing with other people who endured the same trauma experience that made me delve into the emotional impact a family endures when one's health is questionable or impedes someone's ability to earn.

The Quiet Shift

People will sign up for company benefits not realizing they are in place while you work for the company. Rarely does one have portability options. Therefore, if you give your company five to seven years of your life and your protection benefits are tied to your employer, you will lose the benefits and now you are much older. Health plays a major role in protection products. I used my personal story to show Dana what was at stake economically. She was taking all the right steps to accumulate wealth, preservation was critical. At the same time, she was observing her siblings as they navigated through life as families with children. She was becoming more responsible for meeting her mother's economic needs because her siblings felt she had the least amount of responsibility. When it's family, they tend to spend your money before they spend theirs. They will even gang up on you to apply pressure, which is unfair. It allowed us to have multiple serious discussions about what she desired. When someone is in their 20s, they may not necessarily consider being married and having children in their planning process. However, as they see the big 3-0 on the horizon, those considerations begin to take shape.

What exactly do I want out of life? I don't want to remain single forever. I want a home and children. These are the conversations I have with clients, and this is the discussion I had with Dana. She wanted to be more marketable in the workplace, so she opted to pursue her MBA. We chose to protect her life with permanent insurance and add a long-term care option so that her protection benefits would not keep her bound to her existing company. By the time she completed her MBA, she was ready for a change of scenery, so she decided to move from the North to the South. Although love had not yet found her, she was open to it and eventually had

The Quiet Shift

children. She didn't acquire much debt to continue her education. We calculated that if we paid it off and increased her savings systematically, we would remain on track to achieve the financial goal of becoming a millionaire well before retirement. As she began to consider what forty would look like, and her income was increasing, she decided to take the leap and purchase a home. We added a supplemental long-term disability policy to her financial plan as her financial obligations increased and she wanted to maintain the standard of living she has become accustomed to should she ever fall ill. She was still single with no prospects, and she still desired a family.

Life doesn't always pan out the way we envision. Dana did not have any major hiccups in her overall financial planning strategy until she hit forty years old. The first challenge was that she experienced a season of reduced earnings for the first time in her life. Amid Covid-19, her company, like many others, furloughed their employees to manage their company overhead. Initially, it was a reduction of hours, but as the pandemic lingered, it shifted to an unpaid leave of absence. This caused her to consider other employment opportunities, which yielded her a higher income, but she was miserable during a challenging time of isolation. So, she switched jobs only to realize she made a tactical error. Fortunately, she cultivated major relationships in her industry and when an ideal opportunity presented itself, she returned to a previous employer never skipping a financial beat. Add to that, her biological clock was ticking, and she began to realize that she needed to be pragmatic. Covid-19 caused families to come together as a unit for survival's sake. Yet, she didn't have anyone to quarantine with. Yes, she had siblings and a host of nieces and nephews, but she was yearning for more. What if she never had children? Who would care for her as she advanced in age? In anticipation of pursuing her goals and dreams, she was facing the possibility that she may never experience motherhood. Please understand it was not about her overall care and maintenance, she has acquired enough of a net worth to live in comfort for the remainder of her life.

Why am I sharing this? When you begin to focus on wealth accumulation, maintenance, and transference early, you can withstand tumultuous seasons in your life. Now that the pandemic has run its course, Dana is seriously contemplating adoption. Does she have the necessary resources to experience motherhood alone? Yes. Is she still hoping to get married and live happily ever after? She is. But she remains committed to comprehensive planning and uses strategic planning sessions wisely to determine what options she may have should a vulnerability arise. In recognizing she was spending enough resources on her mother's behalf; she secured a life insurance policy on her mother that provided her with comfort in knowing her mom's final wishes would be honored. She has even had conversations with the family about her mom's long-term care needs. However, her greatest priority has always been and remains to live financially free and to leave a legacy to the next generation so that her heirs would not lack.

Falling Short

The privilege of a long life is something to be desired. I can recall getting a phone call from an associate who was asked by her best friend to become her power of attorney. The ironic nature of the situation is that Maxine, the friend of Caroline, has been in her life since they were sixteen years old. Caroline was 95. That made Maxine close in age since they grew up together and made memories over the decades. It is why Caroline trusted Maxine and no one else. But the truth is that both women needed assistance with the activities of daily living. The difference was that Maxine had a support system and Caroline was alone and elderly in this world.

Nevertheless, I entertained the introduction since the conversation was based on Maxine realizing that Caroline needed support that she could not provide. She felt that something was off, things kept happening that she could not explain away. After the introduction, I was able to determine the first stage of dementia was becoming too apparent to ignore. Caroline wasn't the sharp, witty woman of the past who had worked for the state of New Jersey for over forty-five years. Several behavior patterns existed over the years that were detrimentally impacting Caroline at such an advanced age and the maintenance was overwhelming for Maxine.

Caroline was an only child who never truly gravitated to people throughout her life. She was sheltered from the time she was a little girl so making friends was somewhat awkward for her. She met Maxine in school, and they bonded over a love for baking. In home economics, they would talk about growing up, getting married, and doing what they loved most. They saw themselves as successful, happy, and truly enjoying life. Caroline did meet and married a wonderful husband while working for the state as a social worker. However, their union of over fifty years did not bear any children and when he passed away about seven years before the phone call, Caroline had been reduced to only engaging with Maxine consistently.

I have seen a lot over the years, but the Thelma and Louise duo was both heartwarming and heartbreaking. The thought of such a rich, long-lasting friendship does make a spectator reflect upon the beauty of friendship. Yet when reality sets in, they were no longer impressionable teenagers with the strength and energy to conquer the world. The purpose of my visit was to determine how Stanford Angels, LLC might assist with making sure Caroline would live out her final days in comfort. This was a difficult conversation to have because I quickly realized that while Caroline was well-intentioned, she did not manage money well. Having said that, she did make the wise decision to purchase a long-term care policy. When I inquired about what led her to make that decision, it turns out it was based on a conversation she had with a coworker years ago.

Caroline was introduced to the need for long-term care insurance because she watched a coworker exhaust herself attempting to care for her aging parents while maintaining a career. It appeared to be draining the life out of her coworker. Caroline was able to observe the growing bags under her associate's eyes, the sluggish movement, the sparkle disappearing. Caring for the parents looked as if it were a death sentence delivered slowly. One day in conversation, Caroline inquired about the additional responsibilities and her coworker ended the discussion by stating how she wished her parents had invested in long-term care. No one envisioned life becoming so exhausting.

The Quiet Shift

That simple statement resonated so much with Caroline, she went home to share it with her husband that they needed to consider it for themselves. They had both just settled upon the fact that they were not going to have children. It simply never happened and when they looked up, they crossed the big 4-0 threshold. Was it still possible, yes? But they were okay with life as it was.

It is most unfortunate that our mindset immediately goes to the notion that our children will do the right thing when we get older. Long-term care became a necessity for Caroline after she concluded that she was not going to become a mother. She did research recognizing that one day, it would come in handy as the years passed by. The only lens through which that makes sense is realizing that one could grow old and have no one in this world. Statistically speaking, that is a greater possibility for women than men. Whether an individual gives birth to a child or not, if they have siblings growing up or not, if they get married or not, a person can live long enough that everyone else dies before them. What do you do then? We do not have the foresight to determine life expectancy. However, if one were to apply metrics, a woman's life expectancy in the United States for 2021 was 79.1 years and that dropped for the second year in a row. If a person lives to the ripe old age of 90, it is possible that everyone in their support circle did not bode as well. Which is what made Maxine's relationship with Caroline so wonderful.

Getting back to Caroline, she and her husband represented the typical clients who cannot afford to not purchase long-term care. They were socially identified as a middle-class income-producing couple who lived comfortably, but not so fabulous that they did not calculate carefully how they would live out their golden years. They decided the house needed to be paid off before either could retire. By that time, they would have accumulated enough assets to manage taxes and the maintenance of the house. Each had a small retirement nest egg with an average of $200,000. Because Caroline worked for the state, she had a pension in addition to her social security. As residents of the state of New Jersey, they understood they were not eligible for Medicaid based on income-cap limitations. After doing research, they invested but did not solicit the advice of a professional. The goal was to have a care plan in place when they needed assistance in their old age. Just based on Caroline's explanation of her intentions, I could understand she truly didn't understand what she purchased versus what would have been most ideal. She also didn't understand that the cost of long-term care insurance was not fixed. Therefore, over time, the benefits could erode not being enough of the intended benefit. For example, there is a significant difference between simple interest and compounded interest. It would affect the allocated daily benefit amount.

A secondary flawed opinion of Caroline was that it would be a vehicle she could use when she got older for someone to come and care for her. She did not understand there is a medical condition that must underline the ability to tap into the benefit. One must be incapable of performing two out of six activities of daily living. Not based on her struggle, but as defined by a doctor. Finally, she purchased a small service plan which did not translate to many hours daily. Because she was advanced in age, she did manage to get the consent of her physician that she needed help. Yet, when we delved into the details of the policy, it was woefully inadequate. It covered an estimated four hours of service each day. She was well-meaning but did not achieve the goal she set out to accomplish. Caroline was on the right track with her intentions. However, a simple conversation with a professional would have served to be extremely beneficial in her case. Now, her options are extremely limited, and she was forced to live alone with limited help and only Maxine to communicate with.

Speaking of Maxine, it also was not the wisest decision for Caroline to make Maxine her power of attorney. They were best friends since the tender age of 16 and now they are both over ninety years old. Each day on earth is a blessing for them both. If Maxine dies before Caroline, then what? Who handles Caroline's affairs? Growing old is a reality for everyone. It is what we all desire to do because rarely will you find someone who wants to check out of life early in age. Doing so deserves consideration and thought about how you want to live out your golden years. One of the worst experiences imaginable is to be old and frail, incapable of managing your affairs, and falling prey to someone who takes advantage. We have all heard the atrocities of elder abuse and manipulation.

The best antidote for that outcome is a solid strategic plan. Ideally, Caroline had options, especially after her husband died. Realizing she was alone in the world without anyone she could truly rely upon, she could have considered selling her greatest asset-her home. With the proceeds, she could have lived out her golden years in a place secured and filled with other people who may have been all alone in this world as well. Senior communities allow active, self-reliant individuals to enjoy community life.

The Quiet Shift

Many communities offer additional facilities support, which people define as nursing home amenities. An aging individual can set up a plan that allows them to live independently for as long as possible, and then move within the facilities as their health deteriorates over time. With a long-term care policy available, the daily benefit can offset the costs of the facility and provide years of comfort. She would have been able to calculate her options, the type of place she would reside, and who would be entitled to her residual estate. Those options were no longer viable, simply because she did not find the benefit of sitting down with wise counsel.

A Final Act of Love

Just when I was preparing to call Sharon and celebrate the fact that we have honored our assignment, we have finished the course, we have completed the first step in this journey of love, I got this feeling. It took me a moment to quiet my spirit only to realize I had not crossed the finish line. What was missing? We told the stories we were led to share addressing both the emotional and economic impact that affects a family if they do not have critical conversations about aging parents overall. In my sitting still, I recalled the last conversation I had with my mother. We knew the end was near, so everyone gathered at the house. I don't know how we knew she would transition, but on January 8th, 2015, we spent the entire day in and out of her room. We took turns having quiet moments and finally, my siblings left. It was the morning of January 9th. My mom struggled to speak but she insisted on telling me to make sure everyone was alright. Wow! Here we were trying to make certain she was comfortable, she felt free to transition and she was still concerned about the well-being of her daughters.

In my capacity as a CFP®, I serve as a volunteer for various nonprofit organizations. Typically, it's for a specific demographic who may be marginalized or financially devastated and need guidance. However, one nonprofit entity caters to women who desire to be financially free. I was asked to meet with a middle-aged woman who was recently divorced. During the consultation, she shared that she had a son with special needs that she was concerned about. Who would care for him when she died? Immediately I thought about my mother's concern about her daughters as she was taking her last breaths on earth. Most parents are worried about how their children will manage life after they die, especially if they have served as a crutch for their babies life. I can only imagine that a parent with a special needs child has heightened anxiety.

I cannot recall the exact disease of her son, but I do remember that it impacted his muscles causing him to live in a wheelchair. Cognitively, he could contribute to his well-being through instruction and the ability to articulate his level of comfort. He was unable to do anything much thereafter. His parents helped him to function in society as best they could, supporting his desire to attend college and graduate with honors. He was alert. The mother's concern was that she was his primary caregiver and who would undertake that responsibility because she did not want to assume his dad would. His dad had means at the time of the consultation, but he wasn't the most reliable provider and so the prospective client wanted to explore her options.

When a child with special needs receives government benefits, a parent's plan must be specifically crafted to ensure their government medical benefits are not impacted. It requires a comprehensive estate plan to protect your child. Leaving them as the beneficiary on a tax-deferred vehicle or adding their name as a pay-on-death request can disqualify their benefits and the parent will not be able to fight or advocate. In many instances, the amount a disabled person can have in their name is so low, that even a small inheritance can cause massive issues. Add to the fact that it must be reported. For example, SSI recipients have ten days after the end of the month that they received an inheritance to report it to the Social Security Administration, even if they choose to reject the inheritance as the beneficiary.

The Quiet Shift

The best advice I could give that parent was to seek the services of an attorney and do the research to see what her options were. We needed to determine economically, what was possible. But this was food for thought and I wanted to share one strategy that I believe will give parents who fit in this unique circumstance... options. If you really cannot think about anyone willing to take on the responsibility of caring for an adult with special needs, work with an estate attorney to consider establishing a testamentary special needs trust that will provide for your child in a facility that best caters to your child's medical needs. You may be asking; how can I even fund a trust? Insure your life and do it as early as possible. Do not wait until your health is on the decline. It can serve as a fail-stop should the worst possible scenario rear its ugly head. You will have the peace of knowing someone will step in to make sure your child has somewhere to land.

About Dr. Nicole B. Simpson

Reverend Dr. Nicole B. Simpson, CFP® is a practitioner with over 30 years of experience in the securities industry which she entered in 1991 and holds Series 7, 63, and 65 Securities licenses. On September 11, 2001, her life was drastically altered as a financial planner working at 2 World Trade Center on the 73rd floor. Simpson was still in the building on the 44th floor when Tower 2 was hit during the World Trade Center attacks.

Today, Simpson compassionately assists families on how to begin to walk along the road to recovery when faced with a catastrophic, unexpected disaster. She is actively involved in spiritual, emotional, and economic empowerment. A compelling empowerment speaker, television/ radio personality, and author, Ms. Simpson travels throughout the United States teaching in a practical and easy-to-understand manner. Her simple approach motivates everyone who hears her message to take action to change their future. Her commitment is to engage people with the thought, "If money were not an issue, what would be your life's purpose?"

Pastor Nicole's life began to take shape when she turned seven years old. Gifted a bible by her mom she spent most of her time in her room reading the red words in that Bible, sparking her interest. Those red words told her to do good to please God and it taught her how to pray. It was through scripture, she learned how to seek God's comfort amid every storm. Like most individuals, she has suffered an unexpected, significant personal tragedy that affected her entire family emotionally and financially. What is critical, but often avoided, is the experience and willingness to share strategies that instruct others how to overcome unexpected disasters that can stagnate one's personal life because of a crisis. "How does one pick up the pieces of their life and move toward their ordained purpose?" She can answer those questions and put into perspective the necessary steps to begin the recovery process.

In January 2016, she embarked on a new life journey becoming the Pastor of Micah 7 Ministries located in Piscataway, NJ. Her media profile includes appearances on ABC News, CNN News, BBC World News, Huffington Post, Crain's NY Business, Fox News, PBS, and UPN

9. She is a Board Member of the CFP Board Center for Financial Planning Diversity Advisory Group, Chair of the Generation X Community Association, and Provost of the Dare 2 Dream Institute. She frequently speaks on the lecture circuit and has authored several books on financial and life planning. Nicole received a Doctorate in Transformational Leadership with top honors from Boston University, an M.Div. Magna Cum Laude from New Brunswick Theological Seminary, and a B.S. Cum Laude from Oral Roberts University.

After 30 years of industry experience that recognizes an economic cultural reckoning is occurring, Simpson is equipped, realizing she is an anomaly and has much to contribute to the inevitable change America is demanding. This reality demands her to be available as a "teacher, trainer, mentor, guidance counselor".

About Ms. Sharon Stanford

Ms. Sharon Stanford is the owner of Stanford Angels LLC, a home healthcare agency that was founded at the height of the COVID-19 pandemic in 2020. Though a challenging time in the healthcare industry, she persevered and serviced over one hundred people daily for COVID-19 testing and aftercare referrals and services. Founded out of love and concern for the children and seniors throughout the community, she strives to have a long-lasting impact in the years to come by servicing her patients in love and with dignity.

When Sharon is not in the office or taking care of patients, she spends her leisure time with her precious grandchildren, Jakih, Ares, and Iyla. She loves to travel and explore new places with her best friends Talisha and Jorina. She also enjoys experiencing new adventures that include hiking, parasailing, and dancing.

Made in the USA
Middletown, DE
22 June 2023